NEW MERMAIDS

General editors:
William C. Carroll, Boston University
Brian Gibbons, University of Münster
Tiffany Stern, University of Oxford

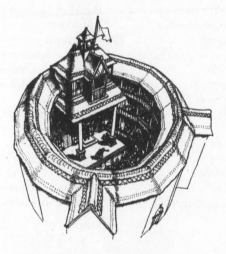

Reconstruction of an Elizabethan theatre
drawn by C. Walter Hodges

NEW MERMAIDS

ARDEN OF FAVERSHAM

Introduction by Tom Lockwood

University of Birmingham

Text edited by Martin White

Professor of Theatre at the University of Bristol

Bloomsbury Methuen Drama
An imprint of Bloomsbury Publishing Plc

BLOOMSBURY

LONDON · OXFORD · NEW YORK · NEW DELHI · SYDNEY

Bloomsbury Methuen Drama
An imprint of Bloomsbury Publishing Plc

Imprint previously known as Methuen Drama

50 Bedford Square	1385 Broadway
London	New York
WC1B 3DP	NY 10018
UK	USA

www.bloomsbury.com

BLOOMSBURY, METHUEN DRAMA and the Diana logo are trademarks
of Bloomsbury Publishing Plc

First New Mermaid edition 1982 published by Ernest Benn Limited
Second Edition with revised introduction published by
Bloomsbury Methuen Drama 2007
Reprinted 2009, 2010, 2013 (twice), 2014, 2016 (twice), 2017

First New Mermaid edition © 1982 Ernest Benn Limited
Second Edition with revised introduction © Bloomsbury Methuen Drama

British Library Cataloguing-in-Publication Data
A catalogue record for this book is available from the British Library.

ISBN: PB: 978-0-7136-7765-2
ePDF: 978-1-4081-4473-2
ePUB: 978-1-4081-4474-9

Library of Congress Cataloging-in-Publication Data
A catalog record for this book is available from the Library of Congress.

Series: New Mermaids

Printed and bound in Great Britain

CONTENTS

ACKNOWLEDGEMENTS

I am particularly grateful to Mr M. P. Jackson for access to his Oxford B. Litt. thesis 'Material for an edition of *Arden of Feversham*' (1963), and I should also like to acknowledge the debt I owe to M. L. Wine's stimulating and scholarly edition in the Revels series (1973).

I have been fortunate enough to direct the play twice — at the University Theatre, Manchester, in 1975, and at the Edinburgh Festival in 1978 — and I should like to thank those concerned for giving me the opportunity to learn about the play in performance.

I am also grateful to Philip Roberts for his initial encouragement and continued interest; to Oliver Neville for his comments on the Introduction; to Brian Gibbons, who saved me from making many an error; and, above all, to Julia Hills for her constant support and help.

Bristol, 1982   MARTIN WHITE

I am grateful to Brian Gibbons for the invitation to write on *Arden of Faversham*, William Carroll for his positive and helpful reading of my Introduction, and to Jenny Ridout and others at A&C Black for their work in seeing the revised edition into print. Teaching the play with Bob Wilcher was crucial in shaping my thinking; Beck, Dan, and Amy were crucial too, but in other ways.

Birmingham, 2007   TOM LOCKWOOD

INTRODUCTION

About the play

Arden of Faversham presents audiences and readers today with a paradox. The real-life events that it stages can be reconstructed from contemporary legal and historical documents with forensic accuracy, but the play that stages them refuses to fit securely within any retrievable theatrical or authorial contexts.[1] On the one hand, there are more than enough pieces of information available for a reconstructive understanding of Thomas Arden's murder in Faversham, Kent, in 1551 at the combined hands of his wife, Alice, and her lover, Mosby, together with their two hired assassins, Black Will and Shakebag, and two local men, Greene and Michael. But, on the other, there seem only too few for a reconstruction of the play's earliest dramatic contexts some time (possibly) in the late 1580s or (more probably) in the early 1590s. This combination of abundant external historical data about a place, a society, and a crime, with minimal information that associates the play with a theatrical company's repertoire or the canon of a known dramatist, has sometimes led critics to write of *Arden of Faversham* as if it were simply a quarry for historical investigation. Indeed the currency and wide dispersal of narratives of Arden's murder in early modern print can sometimes make the play seem but another sensationalising account of an iconic murder.[2] But the play is more than this, on the stage and on the page. *Arden of Faversham* offers, in a thrillingly varied and flexible dramatic language, and in a taut, experimental dramatic form, a series of powerfully realised stagings of issues and ideas that were as live in the early 1590s of the play's probable first performance as they had been in the 1550s when its events took place. The play, among the earliest English domestic tragedies, operates within a wide and challenging set of historical contexts; but it does so only because of its dramatic qualities, and it will be the aim of this introduction to offer an account of the play that keeps its artful theatricality fully in view.

---

1 Patricia Hyde, *Thomas Arden in Faversham: The Man Behind the Myth*, 1996, is the most exhaustive of such reconstructions; fewer materials are gathered with greater theoretical sophistication in Lena Cowen Orlin, *Private Matters and Public Culture in Post-Reformation England*, 1994.

2 The historiography of Arden's narrative is brilliantly treated by Richard Helgerson, 'Murder in Faversham: Holinshed's Impertinent History' in Donald R. Kelley and David Harris Sacks, ed., *The Historical Imagination in Early Modern Britain*, 1997, pp. 133–56.

The plot

The accumulative, overlapping multiple murder plots that constitute *Arden of Faversham* all finally cohere in the tightly described dramatic space and time of Arden's own parlour in Scene XIV; but the play's action has begun before Scene I with Arden's recollection of the attachment between Alice and Mosby; and does not end until its audience has seen the moral and judicial consequences of his murder, and, through Franklin's epilogue, been given a clear sense of the further reach of those consequences outwards from Faversham to Southwark, Flushing and Osbridge and – by extension – the time and location in which they themselves have been witness to the play's action.

The play's long first scene begins with Franklin's confirmation that Arden now possesses lands once belonging to Faversham Abbey; by its close, Alice has canvassed at least four candidates for his murder. The scene establishes the desires and grievances that will animate the play: the incommensurate desires of Michael and Clarke for Mosby's sister, Susan; Arden's dislike of Mosby, and Franklin's role as arbiter; the animus towards Arden displayed by Greene, whose lands Arden has purchased; and Alice's supreme command over these (generally) masculine emotions in the domestic sphere. Scene II introduces Black Will, Shakebag, and Bradshaw, the latter complaining of legal troubles, the two former eager to accept Greene's commission to murder Arden. Scenes III to VII take place in London, and encompass a botched attempt to kill Arden in the street, and the failed attempt by Black Will and Shakebag to murder Arden in his sleep: it having been agreed that they will be let into Arden's lodgings by Michael, their attempt fails when Michael, remorseful in soliloquy (in Scene IV), wakes Arden and Franklin who promptly lock the door Michael was to have left unlocked.

With Scene VIII the play's location returns to Faversham: this, the so-called 'quarrel scene', is at the heart of the play, and of Alice and Mosby's relationship. Within it Mosby moves from canvassing the possibility of murdering her to vowing to follow her 'to the gates of death' (VIII.165); she, similarly, moves from a threat to kill herself, to a renewed sense of their joint undertaking. Scenes IX to XII represent another sequence of failed attempts on Arden's life, the first of which is averted by Lord Cheiny, whose appearance on Rainham Down deprives Black Will and Shakebag of their opportunity to ambush Arden. Black Will and Shakebag again fail to kill Arden when they and he arrive separately at the ferry in Scenes XI and XII, the would-be murderers deprived of their victim by mist, dark, and timing. In Scene XIII, Arden accosts Mosby, who is seen arm-in-arm with Alice, fights with him, and is finally (and fatally) persuaded of Mosby's friendship. He ends the scene intending to offer a reconciliation to Mosby, against Franklin's advice. Scene XIV, Arden's last (but not the play's), gradually gathers the conspirators together in Arden's parlour, rehearses them in the parts they are to play in his murder, and conceals them around the stage in anticipation of his arrival. Once on-stage, Arden plays at dice with Mosby, the game and his life ending at the same time when Black Will and Shakebag jump out at him from their hiding place in the counting house. Mosby and then Alice both also attack the dying Arden, whose body is carried first into the counting house but then, after the arrival of Franklin and his considerable suspicion, into the fields. The scene closes with the entrance of the law in the form of the Mayor and the town watch. After Arden's murder, the play intercuts two soliloquies for the fleeing Shakebag and Black Will (Scenes XV and XVII) with two scenes set in Faversham in which Alice and Mosby are first questioned by the Mayor and then, together with the other conspirators, sentenced to punishment (Scenes XVI and XVIII). Franklin's Epilogue fills in the audience's knowledge of other characters' deaths, and offers a sententious summary of the events they have witnessed and their meaning.

Frontispiece to the 1633 Quarto, illustrating the murder of Arden.

The play

Today's readers and audiences are subject to twin pressures both to situate *Arden of Faversham* within the historical context it so richly realises, and to account for the effects and successes of the play's dramatic structure. Seen historically, *Arden of Faversham* is remarkable for the thoroughness with which it tests its characters, their motivations, and their language within the historicised politics of the family and the locality, overlapping discourses ruptured by Arden's murder, and by the double chronological purchase given a play set in one decade, the 1550s, and probably written and performed in another, the 1590s. This rupture, although it is the enabling condition of the play's existence, can only be fitfully stitched back together by the play's close. In this light the play is set within, and at the same time challenges, a series of powerfully historicised early modern contexts. It explores the issue of women's status within marriage, and the relationships between early modern marriage, the family, and a wider community. By staging the relationship between Alice and Mosby, and the threat it poses to Arden's domestic and local authority, the play examines the tensions between sexuality and transgression. In a related mode, Arden and Franklin's friendship is tested by and within a context of trade, exchange, land-ownership, and contemporary same-sex relationships; Black Will and Shakebag, the two discharged soldiers, returned masterless from continental wars, together charge the play's location with criminality; and the triangular relationship of Michael, Clarke, and Susan refracts and comments on the central adulterous triangle of Alice, Mosby, and Arden from within a context of courtship, exchange, and male authority.

Yet the play never seems as schematic as such a listing might imply. For *Arden of Faversham* is constructed with the special kind of artfulness that can look like apparent artlessness. The sequential stacking of its plots, in which an audience's awareness of the increasingly convoluted threats to Arden's life mounts in apparently inverse proportion to his own ignorance of them, can at times give audiences and readers the impression of childishness, though the tension generated is considerable. For all the complicated consequence of the many murder plots making up the narrative of *Arden of Faversham*, many of the play's audiences have felt themselves in sympathy with Shakebag's protest, late on in the play after yet another failed attempt on Arden's life: 'Zounds, I was ne'er so toiled in all my life / In following so slight a task as this' (XII.48–9). It is part of the contract that *Arden of Faversham* makes with its audience that (in the title Alexander Goehr gave to his operatic adaptation of the play's narrative in 1967) '*Arden Must Die*', for if he did not, the nature of the dramatic truth claimed by its title-page and epilogue would be voided. For this '*Lamentable and True Tragedie*' (as the play's title-page claims), this dramatised account of 'simple truth' (as Franklin claims, Epilogue, line 17), would be evacuated if Arden did not die. But if Arden must die, and an audience must know this, how then can his play generate the tension and suspense necessary to draw in that audience?

William Empson once imagined Shakespeare faced with a similar dramatic predicament. Writing *Hamlet* at the close of the 1590s, Empson thought, Shakespeare must have recognised the problems inherent when writing within a set dramatic form for an audience to whom its narrative shape and, more importantly, its narrative end, must be already known. The situation is analogous to that which must have faced the collaborative authors of *Arden of Faversham* (one of whom, as I explore below, may also have been Shakespeare). As any audience attending Shakespeare's *Hamlet* might be expected to have seen the earlier (now lost) play of *Hamlet*, and to be able to predict the narrative development of the later play from a knowledge of the former, so any audience attending *Arden of Faversham* might be expected to know that Arden would not survive the afternoon's performance, based on a reading of its main source, Holinshed's *Chronicles*, or the many other retellings of Arden's true-life murder. The solution to the *Hamlet*-problem, as Empson imagined Shakespeare imagining it, was 'purely technical'. Since a revenge play, such as *Hamlet*, required its principal revenger to wait until Act 5 before completing the act of revenge with which his narrative tasked him, it also required a means of filling the centre of the play between action and revenge. In Empson's version of Shakespeare's internal monologue:

> He thought: "The only way to shut this hole is to make it big. I shall make Hamlet walk up to the audience and tell them, again and again, 'I don't know why I'm delaying any more than you do; the motivation of this play is just as blank to me as to as it is to you; but I can't help it.'" . . . It turned out, of course, that this method, instead of reducing the old play to farce, made it thrillingly life-like and profound.[3]

Arden of Faversham anticipates the technical solution employed in *Hamlet* in the ongoing commentary of its characters on Arden's increasingly unlikely survival. 'Sirrah Greene, when was I so long in killing a man?', Black Will asks at the start of Scene XIV; 'I think we shall never do it; let us give it over', Greene replies (XIV.1–2). This will be, at last, the scene in which Arden does die; but as the opening exchange in

---

3 William Empson, *Essays on Shakespeare*, 1986, p. 84.

this scene reminds the play's audience again of the delaying tactics that form its central structuring principle, so do they also recall Shakebag's wearied exhalation two scenes earlier ('Zounds, I was ne'er so toiled in all my life': XII.48), and the punctual incredulity of the other would-be murderers after each earlier failed attempt: 'What, dare you not do it?' (III.63), 'Why, sirs, how escaped he?' (IX.139), 'What, is the deed done? Is Arden dead?' (XII.40). At moments such as this, the play, conscious of its slowness, itself voices and anticipates what many audiences feel seeing the play performed; as M. C. Bradbrook writes, they can become 'positively irritated that [Alice] should not succeed' in her wishes.[4] For it is not, of course, that the play cannot kill Arden, but that it has the formal daring to delay his death – to shut the hole by making it big – such that when it does complete its narrative contract in Scene XIV that completion still has the power to surprise. Rather than turn its fidelity to a real-life narrative into a formal restriction, *Arden of Faversham* opens out into delaying, formal innovation within the limits that are imposed by its closed formal structure.

The close connection between murder and dramatic experimentation is seen clearly in the language with which the conspirators describe their enterprise. In the aftermath of Michael's failure of nerve, and failure to deliver the sleeping Arden and Franklin to the dark purposes of Black Will and Shakebag in Scenes IV and V, Shakebag holds him to account:

> Then, Michael, this shall be your penance:
> To feast us all at the Salutation,
> Where we will plot our purpose thoroughly.

> (VII.24–6)

Plot, here, is the modernised form of the verb 'plat', present in all three earlier printed texts of *Arden* (Qq, sig.E3r, all page-for-page reprints). The unmodernised form is attractive for the way it brings together the crucial sense of the modernised *plot* (*OED*, v.2a: 'To plan, contrive, or devise (something to be carried out or accomplished, esp. a crime or conspiracy)' compare *OED*, *plat*, v.41a, 'To plan or devise') with the sound of the homonym *plait*, 'To braid or intertwine' (*OED* v.1a, senses also available for the older spelling *plat*, *OED* v2.2). There are many ways in which the tangled plots of the many conspirators against Arden's life

---

4   M. C. Bradbrook, *Themes and Conventions of Elizabethan Tragedy*, 2nd ed., 1980, p. 40.

do plait together until finally they bind him – literally, in the shape of the towel with which Black Will '*pulls him down*' at XIV.229 s.d. But available, too, is the dramatic sense of *plot*, a term that in the early modern theatre meant not only the planning by its author(s) of a play's action but also a document that hung backstage at each performance giving scene-by-scene details of the play's action, the characters on-stage at any given moment, and sometimes the names of the actors playing those parts.[5] It is easy to imagine such early modern script conferences taking place in venues just like the fictional Salutation to which Shakebag, Black Will, Greene, and Michael are to repair, an ease partly facilitated by the way in which *Arden of Faversham* repeatedly describes the collaborative action of murder in terms that align themselves with the collaborative vocabulary of theatre authors and performers. Only a scene later, Mosby in soliloquy lists 'Michael and the painter too' among those 'Chief actors to Arden's overthrow' (VIII.29–30); and Mosby again, as he for a final time ensures the cooperation of the two hired assassins in the murder, does so in a language that makes them temporarily both characters within the play world's fiction and at the same time actors on the playhouse stage: 'Black Will and Shakebag, will you two / Perform the complot that I have laid?' (XIV.88–9). Such metatheatrical moments remind the play's audience that what they are witnessing is a collaborative fiction, stripping away the effects of stage realism, even as they also remind the audience of the sheer audacity of this plotted performance.

But there are yet two further reasons why the plotting of *Arden of Faversham* is important. The first is that its narrative plot is so consistently focused on a real 'plot of ground', the lands of Faversham Abbey granted to Arden. Reede's complaints in Scene XIII, in which he twice uses the phrase, prophesy a link between Arden's acquisition of the land and his eventual downfall: may, Reede wishes, 'That plot of ground . . . Be ruinous and fatal unto thee!' (XIII.32–4; the earlier use is XIII.12). The play in its Epilogue remembers this moment, and confirms its prescience ('Arden lay murdered in that plot of ground / Which he by force and violence held from Reede': Epilogue, 10–11).[6] The play is thus

---

5 See Grace Ioppolo, *Dramatists and their Manuscripts in the Age of Shakespeare, Jonson, Middleton and Heywood: Authorship, Authority and the Playhouse*, 2006, pp. 31–5, 53–5; David Kathman, 'Reconsidering *The Seven Deadly Sins*', *Early Theatre*, 7 (2004), 13–44, considers one such documentary plot in exemplary detail.

6 This connection is explored in Garrett A. Sullivan, ' "Arden lay murdered in that plot of ground": Surveying, Land, and *Arden of Faversham*', *ELH*, 61 (1994), 231–52; developed and expanded in his *The Drama of Landscape: Land, Property and Social Relations on the Early Modern Stage*, 1998.

bounded from start to finish within this spatial 'plot' and it is bounded, too, by the second further sense of plot, in which Alice's conspiracy within the household is given importance by its analogy to such plots within the nation at large. Exploring that further sense requires us to think about the metaphorical nature of the early modern household.

Published in 1630 (three years before the third quarto of *Arden of Faversham*), Richard Brathwaite's treatise, *The English Gentleman*, gave classic form to the characteristic early modern analogy by which the household was a nation in miniature. 'As every man's house is his Castle,' Brathwaite wrote, 'so is his family a private Commonwealth, wherein if due government be not observed, nothing but confusion is to be expected.'[7] The balancing force of Brathwaite's analogy – 'As . . . so' – both grants power to the male householder and requires of him that it be properly exercised; and it is with the improper setting of this balance that Alice specifically charges Arden in the play, in a language and a rhetorical form that resonate with the terms deployed by Brathwaite:

> If I be merry, thou straightways thinks me light;
> If sad, thou sayest the sullens trouble me;
> If well attired, thou thinks I will be gadding;
> If homely, I seem sluttish in thine eye.
> Thus am I still, and shall be while I die,
> Poor wench abused by thy misgovernment.
>
> (XIII.108–113)

Alice's complaint may be more compelling as a performance for Arden than as an account of the behaviour the play's audience has witnessed to this point; but the orchestration of her speech so that it ends, conclusively, with the political word *misgovernment* is masterfully achieved. Due government unobserved, she seems to say, the expected confusion has arrived; in words that chime with those later used by Brathwaite, Alice describes a domestic commonwealth that has come politically, as well as sexually, apart. But as this political language has moral overtones, so does it also have mortal consequences; for as the nature of the analogy between household and nation meant that they could be legible in the same discourse of political government, so too were they both under the rule of the same law that made a wife's or servant's killing of their

---

7 Richard Brathwaite, *The English Gentleman*, 1630, p. 155; quoted in Catherine Richardson, *Domestic Life and Domestic Tragedy in Early Modern England*, 2006, p. 27, the best recent discussion of the play.

husband or master punishable not simply as murder but as petty treason. Petty treason constructed such a killing as analogous to the killing of the nation's ruler, and was punished as such: hanging for a servant, and burning at the stake for women (as is Alice's sentence: XVIII.30–1).[8] It is for this reason that when Arden describes Mosby as one who 'doth usurp my room' (IV.29) he both recalls Alice's earlier, very different application of the same political figure of usurpation (I.99), and alerts the play's audience to the larger implications of their domestic entanglements. Although only a 'private Commonwealth' (in Brathwaite's phrase), the family could stand as an image of the nation as a whole, in which image transgression of its structures was severely punished; although it does so through the frame of an urban rather than a royal family, *Arden of Faversham* is concerned with precisely the same issues of rule, legitimacy, and national identity as that other great genre of the 1590s, the English chronicle history play.

Seen in this light, *Arden of Faversham* reflects much more of the contemporary nation than its focussed local concerns might at first reveal. For at the same time as *Arden of Faversham* consistently intersects the language of the household with the language of nationhood it is interested, too, in the recursive codes of hospitality that govern (or ought to govern) behaviour among those within the household, and its response towards those who enter it from outside.[9] This is seen most clearly in the parallel between the invitation extended by Lord Cheiny to Arden and Franklin in Scene IX, bidding them (in Black Will's dismissive account) 'to a feast, to his house at Shorlow' (IX.144) and the setting of Arden's murder in Scene XIV. The language in which the earlier invitation is extended, and the language in which Arden, Franklin, and even (surprisingly) Black Will respond to Cheiny, is one that creates and solidifies a discourse of social obligation. All three, however various their precise socio-economic placement in the play, respond to Cheiny in the figure of a binding relationship: Arden considers himself 'Bound to do you service' (IX.101), Franklin 'highly bound to you' (IX.106), and Black Will, obsequiously perhaps and mimicking the two other men, describes himself to Cheiny as 'your beadsman, bound to pray for you' (IX.120). The sense that Cheiny's invitation, the exercise of power through the mechanisms of social interaction, creates a parallel obligation in its

8   Frances E. Dolan, 'Home-Rebels and House-Traitors: Murderous Wives in Early Modern England', *Yale Journal of Law & The Humanities*, 4 (1992), 1–31; and 'The Subordinate('s) Plot: Petty Treason and the Forms of Domestic Rebellion', *Shakespeare Quarterly*, 43 (1992), 317–40.
9   Felicity Heal, *Hospitality in Early Modern England*, 1990.

recipients matters: nowhere in Holinshed's account is such a social gathering proposed, for all that Arden's interchange with his household is made clear; and, though the meal at Lord Cheiny's house is never dramatised, memories of 'the cheer . . . most bounteous and liberal' that it offered are later shared by Franklin and Arden (XIII.67–8). It matters to the play because the invitation, the meal, and the 'divers matters' talked over at it (IX.114) all together recall an older mode of hospitality that was coming under increasing pressure in the period during which the play's events took place, and which was utterly violated by Arden's murder, a crime that has to be committed (in Alice's precise formulation) 'ere the guests come in' (XIV.165). The one, off-stage meal, sets up and sets in relief the two meals that bracket the attempts on Arden's life: the poisoned breakfast of broth (I.360–69) with which Arden begins the play, and the meal which, planned by Arden, is reported by Michael to Alice in Scene XIV:

> . . . my master . . .
> . . . sent me to bring you word
> That Mosby, Franklin, Bradshaw, Adam Fowle,
> With divers of his neighbours and his friends,
> Will come and sup with you at our house this night.
>
> (XIV.34–8)

The guests arrive, of course, only after Arden's murder: little cheer, neither bounteous nor liberal, here. Rather, the collocation of these three social gatherings further emphasises the extent to which the play world in *Arden of Faversham* is one that is no longer capable of sustaining community through the binding obligations that once did structure it, but are – in the play's present – increasingly being moved to the side of daily life.

Spatial figures of speech are often tempting when thinking about *Arden of Faversham* – but, for a play in which the locative is part of its very title, the notion of place in the play is curiously unsettled. *Arden of Faversham* sets in tension the represented world and the representing world, asking an audience or a reader to balance the performed locations of the play world against the real locations in which that performance takes place. The governing metaphor, again, is that of the house: Arden's house and the playhouse, recursively images of one another. When, in Scene XIV, Mosby despairs at Susan and Alice's seeming inability to remove the stain of Arden's blood, his suggested cover-up – 'Why, strew rushes on it, can you not?' (XIV.260) – would have reminded

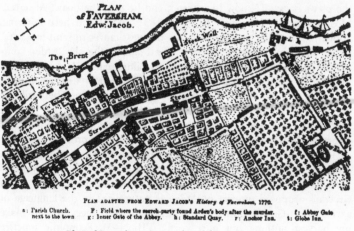

PLAN ADAPTED FROM EDWARD JACOB'S *History of Faversham*, 1770.

a: Parish Church, next to the town P: Field where the search-party found Arden's body after the murder. f: Abbey Gate

K: Inner Gate of the Abbey. h: Standard Quay. r: Anchor Inn. s: Globe Inn.

Plan of Faversham. (Reproduced from Cust, p. 105)

contemporary audiences that rushes were commonly used not only to carpet the floors of domestic spaces but also the stages of playhouses.[10] The same metatheatrical transgression between the represented and the representing world happens in the medium of print whenever the play gestures towards the precincts of St Paul's (as when Arden suggests to Franklin, 'we'll now walk in Paul's / And dine together at the ordinary': VI.41–2). Edward White, the publisher of the first quarto of *Arden of Faversham* in 1592, had his shop 'at the lyttle North dore of Paules Church at the signe of the Gun' (see the facsimile of this title-page on p. 1); the connection between the location that produced the material play text, and the immaterial, fictional world produced by the play text in performance is complicated, but speaks to one of the factors that must account for the play's power: its repeated habit of materially placing itself in the same locations that it also fictionally represents.

Arden of Faversham moves between these material and fictional locations always with the rhythms of trade. Faversham was, through the sixteenth century, an important coasting port for trade goods conveyed from the South-East to London.[11] This knowledge times and pressures

---

10 Andrew Gurr, *The Shakespearean Stage*, 3rd edn, 1992, p. 123.
11 See C. W. Chalkin, 'South-East' and David Harris Sacks and Michael Lynch, 'Ports, 1540–1700' in Peter Clark, ed., *The Cambridge Urban History of Britain, Volume II: 1540–1840*, 2000, pp. 49–66 and 377–424.

the play's days: ''Tis now high water, and he is at the quay', Alice tells Mosby when he asks after Arden (I.183); 'Stand you here loitering, knowing my affairs, / What haste my business craves to send to Kent?', Arden shouts at Michael (III.16–17); and later in the play, Arden commands Michael 'Sirrah, get you back to Billingsgate / And learn what time the tide will serve our turn' (VI.1–2). If the daily tidal rhythms of the coasting trade do not press on the play, then it remembers still the regular flow of men and information in and out of the urban basin of St Paul's churchyard ('I were best shut up my stall,' the Prentice says in Scene III, 'for here will be old filching when the press comes forth of Paul's': III.46–7); and the longer patterns of the local Faversham economy return again when, in his Scene VIII soliloquy, Mosby's thoughts are held in place by the metaphor of the Kent harvest, in which Greene's proposed murder of Arden is naturalised in the language of agriculture ('Greene doth ear the land and weed thee up / To make my harvest nothing but pure corn': VIII.24–5). Economic practice increasingly comes to manage behaviour – and even thought – within the play world.

This business-minded aspect of the play is also one of its most historically-specific aspects. For in the character of Arden, the play at times appears to offer its audience and readers an emblematic case-study of a single man 'greedy-gaping still for gain' (the description is Greene's: I.475), who represents exactly what (in a fine phrase) Keith Wrightson has called 'the acquisitive ambition unleashed in those best placed to exploit the contingencies of the times' in post-Dissolution England.[12] Although the play registers the losses as well as the profits of those who, like Arden, were able to use capital to make a place for themselves in an economic world that, after Henry VIII's dissolution of the monasteries, was now decisively moving away from feudal patterns, *Arden of Faversham* does seem at times centrally concerned with property and possession – possession as, and of, lands, objects, and people. Just as, the play seems to suggest, Arden is able by purchase to take away from Greene the lands near Faversham Abbey 'so that all former grants / Are cut off' (I.461–62), so is Mosby able easily to talk with Clarke later in the same scene of conveying ownership of his sister, Susan, to his possession: 'it resteth at my grant; / You see my sister's yet at my dispose' (I.604–05; although she is tellingly not his to save at XVIII.19–22). This apparent equivalence threatens to dissolve the important distinction offered by

12 Keith Wrightson, *Earthly Necessities: Economic Lives in Early Modern Britain, 1470–1750*, 2002, p. 141.

the early economic historian, William Cunningham, who wrote of the difference between economic relationships, which he thought governed morally by a 'constant regard to the *relations of persons*', and those obtaining in a modern economy, which he thought not morally governed but instead morally neutral, having only to do with 'the *exchange of things*'.[13] For the kinds of commodities in which *Arden of Faversham* trades flicker between moral neutrality and moral charge: land, men, and murder complicate the boundary between persons and things; anything, it seems, can be *granted*, the same discursive figure governing both. Arden himself may be a better trader on the markets than he is a husband, but he is nonetheless held within the play's recognition that the exchange of commodities that make up any trading relationship can also model the personal and emotional exchanges that make up a lived relationship – within a marriage, an extended household, or a community. Arden's gloomy knowledge that 'Love letters pass 'twixt Mosby and my wife' (I.15) is the second textual exchange in the play's first scene, imagining for an audience a personal relationship facilitated by documents that must reflect back upon the handing over by Franklin to Arden of 'the deeds, / Sealed and subscribed' (I.6–7) that confirm Arden's ownership of lands once belonging to the Abbey of Faversham. Love letters and legal letters are crossed in the play's posts, both correspondences entangling people with things.

The language of social intercourse in Faversham is everywhere shot through with the language of commercial exchange: financial metaphors very often structure inter-personal relationships within the play. Examples abound, and in the way in which they permeate the language of all social levels and speakers we see something vital of the connection between Faversham's business and its inhabitants. 'And should I not deal currently with them[?]', Michael asks himself (III.197); Shakebag imagines the 'lazy minutes', 'Loth to give due audit to the hour' (V.7); Mosby figures Arden's wished-for death as the settlement of a business contract, 'Well, were his date complete and expired' (VIII.161); and a whole range of characters are concerned with the way in which the word 'credit' embodies local reputation as a form of financial worthiness (Arden, IV.4; Mosby, VIII.82, 92; Alice, X.85). What we see here in the play is perhaps not so much the spread of the market economy and its language, but rather their internalisation, the growing predominance of fiscal metaphor in personal life.

---

13 Quoted in Wrightson, *Earthly Necessities*, p. 15.

The chain of financial language that links characters and situations through the play is, though, only one of its varied, often startling, linguistic effects, as in Black Will's wonderfully awry demotic ('Give me the money and I'll stab him as he stands pissing against a wall, but I'll kill him', for instance: II.94–5). Consider, as well, the range of social and lexical mobility between the close of Scene IX and the start of Scene X. Defeated in his attempt to murder Arden on Rainham Down by the arrival of Lord Cheiny, Black Will closes his dialogue with his accomplice Shakebag in a demotic, full-rhyme couplet as they decide to report their failure back to Alice: 'Why then let us go and tell her all the matter, / And plot the news to cut him off tomorrow' (IX.152–53). Couplets that close a speech or a scene are not rare in *Arden of Faversham* – they can extend even to the semantically and aurally bathetic rhyme of 'silly man' with 'Endymion' given to Alice at XIV.149–50 – but the rasp of Black Will's rhyme is only further pointed by the immediately altered lexicon given to Arden, talking with Michael, Franklin, and Alice, whose expected displeasure ('how she'll chafe when she hears of this!' IX.150) has been so vividly anticipated by the closing of the previous scene. It is not displeasure that an audience hears as the staged action reverts to Arden's house, however, but description:

See how the Hours, the guardant of heaven's gate,
Have by their toil removed the darksome clouds,
That Sol may well discern the trampled pace
Wherein he wont to guide his golden car.

(X.1–4)

This is, oddly, non-dramatic poetry, much more akin to the rhetorical, classical display of Elizabethan verse written for readers rather than a theatre audience; indeed, it is far removed from the abrupt, functional language more often given to Arden in the play.[14] In context, we see this clearly, as the scene is soon quickened into the business of making the play's plot work by the taciturn, more characteristic clauses of Arden's next line ('The season fits; come, Franklin, let's away': X.5), but for its first four lines the changed, classically-allusive register of Arden's description slows the play's forward progression, even as it describes the coming of a new day, the day that had been the 'tomorrow' of Black Will's speech. Yet the four lines that open Scene X are not

14 The distinction between non-dramatic and dramatic language is one developed at length in Frank Kermode, *Shakespeare's Language*, 2000.

uncharacteristic of other moments in the play. The similar speech with which Shakebag opens Scene V – 'Black night hath hid the pleasures of the day, / And sheeting darkness overhangs the earth . . .': V.1–2) – was judged by at least one production, Terry Hands' in 1982–3 for the RSC, so purely descriptive that it was delivered as an amplified voice-over rather than in character on the stage.

This fluidity of linguistic register is also a measure of the play's way with language as an index of character and social status.[15] Partly this is evident in the busy de-mobbed life of energetic (and exaggerated) gangsterism recalled by Black Will: after service under 'the king at Boulogne' (IX.24), he now employs himself in the pursuit of protection rackets, inventive revenge, and civic violence (XIV.5–27); once fixed in legality by his royal service, Black Will is, after his remove, as linguistically forceful as he is illegally active. Partly too this concern is evident in Arden and Alice, who, although they no longer share in many senses a marriage, share a common vocabulary. When Alice, furious with Mosby in the play's long first scene, sends him away – 'Base peasant, get thee gone' (I.198) – she picks up to throw at him the same adjective that Arden had earlier associated with Mosby in his (and the play's) first description of him:

> A botcher, and no better at the first,
> Who, by base brokage getting some small stock,
> Crept into service of a nobleman
>
> (I.25–7)

Base is twice again in Arden's mouth later in the scene in his angry exchanges with Mosby. 'She's no companion for so base a groom,' he says of Alice (I.305); twenty lines later, Arden calls Mosby 'a velvet drudge, / A cheating steward, and base-minded peasant' (I.322–23), putting together in his final insult the same pair of words earlier used by Alice. Indeed, it is the measure of Arden's mistaken trust in Mosby's innocence that he asks Mosby to forget 'the base terms I gave thee late' (I.341). The connections that link the language of husband and wife – as seen again in their shared fear of a public shame, legible (as they imagine) on their engraved foreheads at IV.16–17 and VIII.76 – cut against the emotional and political links they have to others in the play's action. Language is a

---

15 Michael Neill, ' "This Gentle Gentleman": Social Change and the Language of Status in *Arden of Faversham*', *Medieval and Renaissance Drama in England*, 10 (1998), 73–97.

sensitive register of their residual affection, even as it is a measure of the distance growing between them.

Alice herself recognises as much: 'marriage is but words', she says, alone on the stage in Scene I (I.101), the first of a number of similar locutions in which she reaches for linguistic mutability as a defence for her sexual and emotional departures from Arden. 'Oaths are words, and words is wind, / And wind is mutable', she will say again before the scene's end, snatching time among the business of exits and entrances to be together with Mosby (I.436–7). Tellingly, Mosby is much less linguistically able or daring than Alice ('yet, by your leave, / I'll keep mine unbroken', he replies: I.439–40): it is her particular claim within the play that a freedom of sexual choice, and a disdain for the formal, socially recognised structures of marriage, can be founded on an understanding of language radically at odds with those around her. Does Alice speak to and for a kind of possibility for agency and empowerment that is greater than the play's treatment of it? The potential (and actual) disruption of such claims are policed carefully by the play's narrative: is it rather, then, that Alice represents not a dissident and destabilising perspective within the text and its society, but rather an instance of what scholars have called ventriloquism, a feminine voice within the text actually mouthing lines and positions created by a male author?[16] In some ways it is tempting to see the play simply emptying out Alice's claims for agency and action – emptying them out both because of what she does in its narrative, and because of the way in which she makes them. But the play is her tragedy in some ways as much as it is Arden's: hers is the role that stands at the centre of so many scenes, a virtuoso part for the boy actor who would have played her on the Elizabethan stage. Like the character of Alice herself, the boy actor, as Stephen Orgel and David Kathman have reminded us, was implicated in a series of economic contexts that shade into the social; and the erotic energies potentially released in the theatre by the body of the cross-dressed boy add further charge to the relationships at the centre of the play.[17] Nowhere are these contrasting, and sometimes contradictory, features of Alice and the play more apparent than in performance.

16 Elizabeth D. Harvey, *Ventriloquized Voices: Feminist Theory and English Renaissance Texts*, 1992.
17 Stephen Orgel, *Impersonations: The Performance of Gender in Shakespeare's England*, 1996; David Kathman, 'Grocers, Goldsmiths, and Drapers: Freemen and Apprentices in the Elizabethan Theatre', *Shakespeare Quarterly*, 55 (2004), 1–49.

The play in performance

The history of *Arden of Faversham* in the professional as in the amateur theatre is discontinuous. We have no record of the location or company associated with the first performance of *Arden of Faversham*, a situation that, regrettably, is far from unique for plays on the early modern stage. Later evidence is imperfect, and so inconclusive, but Roslyn Knutson's suggestion that *Arden of Faversham* seems likely to have moved from the ownership of Pembroke's Men in the early 1590s and into the repertory of the Chamberlain's Men after 1594 largely has been accepted by scholars.[18] The likelihood of any later productions in the sixteenth century is a matter of similar conjecture. Knutson has proposed that play texts were commonly printed within a year or two of their being successfully revived in the theatre repertory; if she is right, the 1599 quarto might signal the play's participation, both through performance and through print, in what was at the close of the century a boom period for domestic tragedy on the stage. In this period the Admiral's Men acquired a set of three such plays – *Page of Plymouth*, *Cox of Collumpton*, and *The Tragedy of Thomas Merry* – and the Chamberlain's Men probably also performed *A Warning for Fair Women*: it is a grouping with which *Arden of Faversham* interestingly interacts.[19] No documentary evidence has, however, surfaced that would confirm this tempting hypothesis.

In subsequent centuries, *Arden of Faversham* has regularly been revived, but without ever coming to stand centrally in the theatrical repertoire. An adaptation of the play by George Lillo, probably completed by John Hoadley at some point after Lillo's death in 1739, saw only a single performance at Drury Lane on 12 July 1759; printed in 1762, the Lillo-Hoadley *Arden* represents a radical (if clearly unsuccessful) reshaping of the play's narrative materials, but one consistent with a hope that such 'A dreadful story of domestic woes' (as the anonymous Prologue puts it) could have continued commercial success.[20] More recently, the play has over the past forty years been irregularly revived on stage. Two productions coincided chronologically if not geographically

---

18 Roslyn L. Knutson, 'Shakespeare's Repertory' in David Scott Kastan, ed., *A Companion to Shakespeare*, 1999, pp. 346–61; compare Andrew Gurr, *The Shakespeare Company, 1594–1642*, 2004, pp. 127–33, whose *The Shakespearian Playing Companies*, 1996, clarifies their institutional histories.

19 Roslyn L. Knutson, *The Repertory of Shakespeare's Company, 1594–1613*, 1991, pp. 12–13, 68.

20 George Lillo, *Arden of Feversham*, 1762; H. Diack Johnstone, 'Four Lost Plays Recovered: *The Contrast* and Other Dramatic Works of John Hoadley (1711–1776)', *The Review of English Studies*, 57 (2006), 487–506.

in 1978, the play being twice produced that summer and autumn in Edinburgh and Mold; more recently, the play has been twice chosen for amateur production in University theatres, as at the Little Theatre, Auckland (1984), and the School of Drama, Victorian College of the Arts, Melbourne (1999).[21] Larger productions include that directed by Buzz Goodbody at the Roundhouse in 1970. Michael Billington, reviewing the production for *The Times*, complained that it 'never matches the topographical precision of the original, making absolutely no scenic distinction between London streets and the Kentish countryside', but felt that the performance of Dorothy Tutin as Alice justified the revival.[22] Billington's praise for Tutin was echoed by other reviewers, although more than one chimed with Nicholas De Jongh's words in *The Guardian* in finding, with adjectival caution, that the 'interest of this brave revival ... is how an unwieldy text translates to the stage'.[23] The production directed by Terry Hands for the Royal Shakespeare Company at The Other Place, Stratford, in 1982 (subsequently transferring to the Gulbenkian Theatre, Newcastle-upon-Tyne and to the RSC repertoire at the Pit Theatre, London) followed the pattern established by Goodbody's production in having at its centre a star actress, in this case the young Jenny Agutter, making her debut at Stratford.[24] In the twenty-first century, *Arden* has been adapted for radio performance by John Tydeman (first broadcast on BBC Radio 3, 6 June 2004); the same year saw also a production in New York at the Metropolitan Playhouse (16 April–15 May). It is to be hoped that recent claims for the partly Shakespearean authorship of the play, discussed below, will be tested by future revivals.

One final feature of the play's performance history is the tradition of its being performed actually in Faversham. Faversham had a thriving theatrical culture in the sixteenth century, with regular recorded visits from the major London companies on tour, though no record survives of *Arden of Faversham* being performed in the town for this period.[25] Later records do, though, indicate that the play was regularly performed in

---

21 These details are taken from the annual census of productions offered each year in *Research Opportunities in Renaissance Drama*, which also lists reviews where available.

22 Michael Billington, 'Arden of Faversham', *The Times*, 6 November 1970.

23 Nicholas de Jongh, 'Arden', *The Guardian*, 6 November 1970; other useful reviews include Anthony Curtis, *Financial Times*, 7 November 1970, and P.W.B., *The Stage* 12 November 1970.

24 John Barber, 'Refreshing, this witch with murder in mind', *Daily Telegraph*, 31 March 1982; other useful reviews include Michael Coveney, *Financial Times*, 31 March 1982, and Jenny Rees, *Daily Express*, 31 March 1982.

25 James M. Gibson, ed., *Kent: Diocese of Canterbury*, Records of Early English Drama (REED), 3 vols, 2002.

Faversham itself at least from the eighteenth century. Edward Jacob, himself a resident, complained in 1770 that the inhabitants of Faversham too regularly put on amateur productions of the play: they had, he moaned, 'till of late, at a few Years interval, doubly murdered it, by the excessive bad Manuscript Copies they used, and their more injudicious acting; to the no small Discredit of this valuable Tragedy'.[26] It is curious to note the extent to which Jacob's own editorial work on the play (see below) caused him to internalise its language and subject matter in his own prose (the metaphors of murder and credit), but hard to give precise evidence to support his complaints. For although, in fact, one eighteenth-century manuscript text of the play is extant, part of a larger manuscript collection compiled by Thomas Southouse, an antiquary from Kent, it is more probably derived from an earlier literary transcript of the play rather than directly from any early printed text, or any text immediately associated with performance.[27] The Southouse manuscript of *Arden of Faversham* does, however, contain a Prologue and Epilogue to the play, the former dated 1716: neither are sophisticated, either stylistically or conceptually; and may also suggest something of the quality of any performance with which they were associated, as these lines from the Prologue intimate:

> So we presume to Actt a tradgedy
> Its Ardens Tradgedy, a Story sad
> Nothing is worse, the Actters are as bad.[28]

The play's eighteenth-century association with local performance was recently revived by a company of amateur actors who, on 30 August 2000, performed the play at Arden's House in Faversham under the direction of Ian Garner, if only with limited success.[29]

Note on the text
Edward White entered 'The tragedie of Arden of Feuersham & blackwill' in the Stationers' Register on 3 April 1592, and the quarto playbook on which the text of this New Mermaids edition is based was printed for

---

26 Edward Jacob, ed., *The Lamentable and True Tragedie of M. Arden of Faversham*, 1770, p. iv.

27 J. M. Nosworthy, 'The Southouse Text of *Arden of Feversham*', *The Library*, 5th ser., 5, (1950–51), 113–29.

28 J. M. Nosworthy, 'The Southouse Text of *Arden of Feversham*', 127.

29 Review by Ian Shuttleworth for *www.ft.com*, 30 August 2000; now available at www.compulink.co.uk/~shutters/.

him, probably by the London printer Edward Allde, later in the same year; a facsimile of the title-page of this first quarto edition is given on p. 1. The nature of the text printed for White, and so the nature of the manuscript from which the compositor worked, has been the subject of dispute and is still not resolved to universal satisfaction; if, as seems likely, the play was the result of collaboration between two or more dramatists, it may be in fact that the manuscript made available to Allde's printing house was itself various in nature and form. Two further early modern editions of *Arden of Faversham* appeared before the closing of the theatres in 1642: the second quarto in 1599 is a simple reprint of the first; but the third quarto of 1633 is a more ambitious repackaging of the play to new potential audiences. Both the first and second quarto of the play are set in what is known as 'black-letter', a typographical choice that indicates something (although not all) of the two books' publishers' aims for them.[30] However similar the two playbooks, the very fact that a second quarto was printed within such a relatively short time tells us something important about the play's commercial success in print during a period in which relatively few play texts were reprinted, and possibly also something of *Arden of Faversham*'s early theatrical history, as we have seen.[31] The third quarto, much later, resets the play in roman type, which, by then, was the dominant font for playbook publishing; it is also the only one of the three early quartos to include the now-iconic woodcut engraving of Arden's murder (illustrated on p. ix).[32] In fact, Q1633 shares this image with an undated but surely contemporary broadside ballad, *The complaint and lamentation of Mistresse Arden of Faversham*, in which the lively couplets of Alice's lament are sung to the tune of 'Fortune my foe'. Indeed, it might better be said that the third quarto borrows the image from the broadside, since in the broadside the image sits solidly, on the horizontal, across the heads of the two left-hand columns of this four-column, single-sheet text; in the quarto, by contrast,

30 Zachary Lesser, 'Typographic Nostalgia: Play-Reading, Popularity, and the Meanings of Black Letter' in Marta Straznicky, ed., *The Book of the Play: Playwrights, Stationers, and Readers in Early Modern England*, 2006, pp. 99–126; Lesser's book, *Renaissance Drama and the Politics of Publication: Readings in the English Book Trade*, 2004, explores some of the reasons for, and expectations with which, publishers published early modern plays.

31 Knutson, *The Repertory of Shakespeare's Company, 1594–1613*, p. 68; on the printing of playbooks more generally see Peter Blayney, 'The Publication of Playbooks' in John D.Cox and David Scott Kastan, eds, *A New History of Early English Drama*, 1997, pp. 383–422.

32 The image is usefully discussed in R. A. Foakes, *Illustrations of the English Stage, 1580–1642*, 1985.

the image runs vertically up the verso of the playbook's title-page, necessitating an awkward rotation of the book to bring it into viewing line. Again, questions might be asked about the possible intended audiences for these two contemporary publications, the broadside in its old-fashioned black-letter type perhaps addressing a more popular and financially less well-off audience than the modern-looking, roman-set playbook; but as is so often the case with *Arden of Faversham*, the connections created by the shared woodcut serve to complicate any such easy distinction.

Martin White, who edited the text of this New Mermaids edition, made a number of alterations to the text as printed in the 1592 quarto, all in keeping with the editorial policies of the series: the edited text sets much of what is printed as verse in Q1592 as the prose it more properly seems to be; it modernises and rationalises the quarto's punctuation, sometimes indiscriminate and almost certainly non-authorial; and it extends and adjusts the stage directions and speech headings of Q1592 in order to clarify stage action (any such changes are recorded within [square brackets]). The early texts of *Arden of Faversham* do not divide it by acts but only scene, as is the practice here. Any substantive emendations to the text of Q1592 are recorded in the notes to the word or passage in question; the abbreviation 'ed.' does not refer to any individual, named editor, but rather to the editorial tradition as a whole.

Date and sources

The main source for *Arden of Faversham* is also our main help in dating it: the account of Arden's murder given in the second edition of Raphael Holinshed's *Chronicles of England, Scotland and Ireland*, published in 1587, and whose marginalia in particular seem to have inspired particular moments in the play's action, marks the point before which the play cannot have been written.[33] The full text of Holinshed's account is printed as the appendix to this edition; and by putting this narrative in parallel with the action of the play it is clear that the adjustments of, and additions to, this source material are sure and expert. The assurance of the authorial shaping by which the historical record is fashioned into the dramatic syntax of the play is seen most readily in the additions to the play's source material: the second triangular relationship between Clarke, Michael, and Susan, set in parallel to, and reflecting on, the central

33 M. L. Wine, ed., *Arden of Faversham*, Revels Plays, 1973, pp. xl–xli.

adulterous triangle of Arden, Mosby, and Alice; and the creation of Franklin, whose very name associates him with a mode of independent, open hospitality and social place entirely at odds with the obligations and suspicions operative elsewhere in this dramatised Faversham.[34] Where the older triangle of Arden, Mosby, and Alice reflects back on the miseries of failed marriage, their younger counterparts, Michael, Clarke, and Susan, are put in competition by their anticipation of marriage. The parallelism of interest between the two pairings is matched by the repeated patterns of stage action that also link them: the blow of Clarke's with which '*he breaks* MICHAEL's *head*' (X.72s.d.), anticipates the action implied as Mosby takes his part in the eventual murder of Arden ('There's for the pressing iron you told me of', he mutters, as he strikes him: XIV.232).

Part of Franklin's purpose in the play is purely functional, a dramatised voice within the play world who can pass judgement during and after it in ways akin to those judgements passed by other early modern commentators on Arden's murder.[35] Among the most virulent of such commentators, Thomas Beard wrote with satisfied hostility of the punishments meted out on Arden's killers: 'thus all the murderers had their deserved dewes in this life, and what they endured in the life to come (except they obtaine mercy by true repentance) it is easie to judge.'[36] Even the play's first title-page weighs in on 'the vnsatiable desire of filthie lust and the shamefull end of all murderers' (see p. 1). The Epilogue spoken by Franklin is more careful than this, for it accommodates a stylistic defence of this 'naked tragedy' (line 14) alongside its record of justice visited, and indeed by the way in which the heterosexual pull between Arden and Alice is measured by the homosocial painting of the relationship between Arden and Franklin. The language of male relationships, and expectations of what they might entail, were different in the early modern period from our own.[37] Franklin, Arden's 'honest friend' (IX.104) in a play where neither word is weightless, is both a business associate and a companion. Alice presents herself as loath to lose her

---

34 Spenser's Red Crosse knight encounters 'a francklin faire and free' in the House of Holiness in Book 1 of *The Faerie Queene*, 1590, 1.x.6; the domestic circumstances of the play's Franklin have altered rather.

35 The larger questions attendant on this distinction are canvassed by Stephen Orgel, 'What is a Character?', in his *The Authentic Shakespeare and Other Problems of the Early Modern Stage*, 2002, pp. 7–14.

36 Thomas Beard, *The Theatre of God's Judgements*, 1597, p. 271; u/v and i/j regularised.

37 See Eve Kosofsky Sedgwick, *Between Men: English Literature and Male Homosocial Desire*, 1985; Paul Hammond, *Figuring Sex Between Men from Shakespeare to Rochester*, 2002.

husband to his business in the city with Franklin ('Wilt thou to London, then, and leave me here?': I.400) but her loss is measured by the choice any production – or reader – of the play must make in deciding what tone and weight to give to Franklin's balancing line: 'Then stay with me in London; go not home' (IV.28). The indirections of loyalty and desire in this relationship are brilliantly played out in Alice's stage direction two-thirds of the way through the long first scene: '*And then she kisseth him*' (I.411s.d.). Kisses, that is, Franklin, rather than her husband, 'In hope,' as she says, 'you'll hasten him home' (I.411). Alice is performing to an on- as well as an off-stage audience, but it is the playwright(s)' addition of Franklin to the source material found in Holinshed that has made this moment possible.

The author(s)

Scholars of the early modern theatre are increasingly recovering a full sense of what must have been evident to all involved in the writing, production, and performance of the plays in their original contexts: that early modern plays are radically collaborative.[38] In this, *Arden of Faversham* is likely to have been typical of its contemporaries; but the evidence for its collaborative typicality is as yet fragmentary, and has been subject to long-running scholarly investigation (and dispute) at least since the eighteenth century. In some ways the most recent piece of evidence is the firmest, and the one that looks likely to set studies of the play on a new footing in the coming years: MacDonald P. Jackson's convincing demonstration, after a career-long advocacy of the case, that the author responsible for Scene VIII, the 'quarrel scene' between Alice and Mosby, was William Shakespeare.[39] Jackson demonstrates the continuities between this part of *Arden of Faversham* and Shakespeare's other works (and offers, too, a wonderfully nuanced close-reading of the scene); and Jackson's work reveals further, if further proof were needed, the relative murkiness of our sense of the authorship of the other parts of the play not claimed by him for Shakespeare. That Jackson's is only a partial claim for Shakespearean authorship in *Arden of Faversham* distances it from a tradition that since the eighteenth century has claimed Shakespeare as the play's sole author; Edward Jacob's 1770 edition of the

---

38 Brian Vickers, *Shakespeare Co-Author*, 2002; Vickers' appendix is highly critical of Jeffrey Masten's earlier, provocative *Textual Intercourse: Collaboration, Authorship, and Sexualities in Renaissance Drama*, 1997.

39 MacDonald P. Jackson, 'Shakespeare and the Quarrel Scene in *Arden of Faversham*', *Shakespeare Quarterly*, 57, (2006), 249–93.

play, printed in and dedicated from Faversham itself, was the first to test (insufficiently, we might now think) the 'Proposition' that *Arden* might be Shakespeare's 'earliest theatrical Production now remaining'.[40] It is to be hoped that scholars will take up the invitation to new work on the authorship of the play extended by Jackson's article.

---

40 Edward Jacob, ed., *The Lamentable and True Tragedie of M. Arden of Faversham*, 1770, p. iii.

FURTHER READING

David Attwell, 'Property, Status, and the Subject in a Middle-Class Tragedy: *Arden of Faversham*', *English Literary Renaissance*, 21 (1991), 328–48.

Frances E. Dolan, *Dangerous Familiars: Representations of Domestic Crime in England, 1500–1700*, 1994.

Diana E. Henderson, 'The Theater and Domestic Culture' in John D. Cox and David Scott Kastan, eds., *A New History of Early English Drama*, 1997, pp. 173–94.

Patricia Hyde, *Thomas Arden in Faversham: The Man Behind the Myth*, 1996.

MacDonald P. Jackson, 'Shakespearean Features of the Poetic Style of *Arden of Faversham*', *Archiv für das Studium der neueren Sprachen und Literaturen*, 230 (1993), 279–304.

idem, 'Shakespeare and the Quarrel Scene in *Arden of Faversham*', *Shakespeare Quarterly*, 57 (2006), 249–93.

Peter Lake, 'Deeds Against Nature: Cheap Print, Protestantism and Murder in Early Seventeenth Century England', in Kevin Sharpe and Peter Lake, eds., *Culture and Politics in Early Stuart England*, 1994, pp. 257–84.

Alexander Leggatt, '*Arden of Faversham*', *Shakespeare Survey 36*, 1983, 121–33.

Randall Martin, ' "Arden Winketh at his Wife's Lewdness, & Why!": A Patrilineal Crisis in *Arden of Faversham*', *Early Theatre*, 4 (2001), 13–33.

Subha Mukherji, 'Women, Law, and Dramatic Realism in Early Modern England', *English Literary Renaissance*, 35 (2005), 248–72.

Lena Cowen Orlin, *Private Matters and Public Culture in Post-Reformation England*, 1994.

Catherine Richardson, *Domestic Life and Domestic Tragedy in Early Modern England*, 2006.

Wendy Wall, *Staging Domesticity: Household Work and English Identity in Early Modern Drama*, 2002.

Frank Whigham, *Seizures of the Will in Early Modern English Drama*, 1996.

Keith Wrightson, *Earthly Necessities: Economic Lives in Early Modern Britain, 1470–1750*, 2002.

ABBREVIATIONS

ed.	editor
n.	note
O.E.D.	*Oxford English Dictionary*
Q1	First Quarto 1592
Q2	Second Quarto 1599
Q3	Third Quarto 1633
Qq	the first three quartos (Q1, Q2, Q3)
s.d.	stage direction
s.p.	speech prefix
Adams	H. H. Adams, *English Domestic Or, Homiletic Tragedy 1575 to 1642,* New York, 1943.
Bluestone	Max Bluestone, 'The Imagery of Tragic Melodrama in *Arden of Feversham*', in M. Bluestone and N. Rabkin (eds.), *Shakespeare's Contemporaries,* Second Edition, New Jersey, 1970. Reprinted from *Drama Survey,* Vol. 5 (1966), 171–81.
Chapman	Raymond Chapman, '*Arden of Feversham*: Its Interest Today' *English,* XI (1956), 15–17.
Cust	Lionel Cust, '*Arden of Feversham*', *Archaeologica Cantiana,* XXXIV (1920), 101–126.
Holinshed	Ralph Holinshed, *The Chronicles of England, Scotland, and Ireland,* 2nd edition, 1587.
Jackson	M. P. Jackson, 'Material for an edition of *Arden of Feversham*', unpubl. B. Litt. thesis, Oxford, 1963.

Johnson   Samuel Johnson, *A Dictionary of the English Language*, 1755.

Ousby   Ian Ousby and Heather Dubrow Ousby, 'Art and Language in *Arden of Faversham*', *Durham University Journal*, Vol. LXVIII 1, (New Series Vol. XXXVII No. 1), December 1975, 47–54.

Sugden   E. H. Sugden, *A Topographical Dictionary to the Works of Shakespeare and His Fellow Dramatists*, 1925.

Tilley   M. P. Tilley, *A Dictionary of the Proverbs in England in the Sixteenth and Seventeenth Centuries*, Ann Arbor, 1950.

Youngblood   Sarah Youngblood, 'Theme and Imagery in *Arden of Feversham*', *Studies in English Literature*, III (1963), 207–218.

KEY

THE
LAMENTA=
BLE AND TRVE TRA-
GEDIE OF M. AR-
DEN OF FEVERSHAM
IN KENT.

Who was most wickedlye murdered , by
the meanes of his disloyall and wanton
wyfe, who for the loue she bare to one
Mosbie, hyred two desperat ruf-
fins Blackwill and Shakbag,
to kill him.

Wherin is shewed the great mal-
lice and discimulation of a wicked woman, the vnsatiable desire of filthie lust
and the shamefull end of all
murderers.

Imprinted at London for Edward
White, dwelling at the lyttle North
dore of Paules Church at
the signe of the
Gun. 1592.
❋

[DRAMATIS PERSONAE

IN ORDER OF APPEARANCE

ARDEN
FRANKLIN, *his friend*
ALICE, *Arden's wife*
ADAM FOWLE, *landlord of the Flower-de-Luce*
MICHAEL, *Arden's servant*
MOSBY
CLARKE, *a painter*
GREENE
SUSAN, *Mosby's sister and Alice's servingmaid*
BRADSHAW, *a goldsmith*
BLACK WILL ⎱ *hired murderers*
SHAKEBAG ⎰
A PRENTICE
LORD CHEINY, *and his* MEN
A FERRYMAN
DICK REEDE
A SAILOR, *his friend*
MAYOR OF FAVERSHAM, *and the* WATCH]

SCENE I

Enter ARDEN *and* FRANKLIN

FRANKLIN

    Arden, cheer up thy spirits and droop no more.
    My gracious Lord the Duke of Somerset
    Hath freely given to thee and to thy heirs,
    By letters patents from his majesty,
    All the lands of the Abbey of Faversham.   5
    Here are the deeds,
    Sealed and subscribed with his name and the king's.
    Read them, and leave this melancholy mood.

ARDEN

    Franklin, thy love prolongs my weary life;
    And, but for thee, how odious were this life,   10
    That shows me nothing but torments my soul,
    And those foul objects that offend mine eyes;
    Which makes me wish that for this veil of heaven
    The earth hung over my head and covered me.
    Love letters pass 'twixt Mosby and my wife,   15
    And they have privy meetings in the town.
    Nay, on his finger did I spy the ring
    Which at our marriage day the priest put on.
    Can any grief be half so great as this?

FRANKLIN

    Comfort thyself, sweet friend; it is not strange   20
    That women will be false and wavering.

ARDEN

    Ay, but to dote on such a one as he
    Is monstrous, Franklin, and intolerable.

---

  2 *Duke of Somerset* Edward Seymour, the Duke of Somerset, (born c. 1506) was appointed
    Lord Protector in 1547, on the accession of Edward VI (*his majesty*, 1. 4), at the age of
    nine. Somerset was executed in 1552.
  4 *letters patents* Open letters or documents, usually from a sovereign, conferring some
    right, title, property or office.
 11 *shows* affords
 13 *for this veil of heaven* instead of the sky
 15 *pass* ed. (past Qq)

FRANKLIN

Why, what is he?

ARDEN

A botcher, and no better at the first, 25
Who, by base brokage getting some small stock,
Crept into service of a nobleman,
And by his servile flattery and fawning
Is now become the steward of his house,
And bravely jets it in his silken gown. 30

FRANKLIN

No nobleman will count'nance such a peasant.

ARDEN

Yes, the Lord Clifford, he that loves not me.
But through his favour let not him grow proud,
For were he by the Lord Protector backed,
He should not make me to be pointed at. 35
I am by birth a gentleman of blood,
And that injurious ribald that attempts
To violate my dear wife's chastity—
For dear I hold her love, as dear as heaven—
Shall on the bed which he thinks to defile 40
See his disseevered joints and sinews torn,
Whilst on the planchers pants his weary body,

---

25 *botcher* 'A mender of old clothes; the same to a tailor as a cobbler to a shoemaker' (Johnson).

at the first in his origins (Sturgess)

26 *base brokage* 1. pimping (see I.604–7) 2. shady business deals

29 *steward* The official who controlled the domestic arrangements of a large household, and, therefore, a position of importance and responsibility.

30 *bravely jets it* ostentatiously swaggers about
silken gown A gown, chain, and white staff were the insignia of a steward's office.

32 *Lord Clifford* In fact, according to Holinshed, Mosby was the servant of Sir Edward (later Lord) North, Alice's step-father and Arden's former master. No mention is made of these facts in the play, however, and the fictional 'Lord Clifford' is substituted. Cust (p. 114) suggests that the alteration was 'probably made to prevent scandal in the North family.' Sir Thomas North, Alice's step-brother and the translator of Plutarch, was still alive when the play was printed.

33 *his* i.e. Lord Clifford's *him* i.e. Mosby

36 *gentleman of blood* 'One who is entitled to bear arms, though not ranking among the nobility' (*O.E.D.*). See I.310–11.

37 *injurious* insulting, slanderous
ribald Q3 (riball Q1–2). 1. base fellow 2. lewd, wanton

42 *planchers* floor boards

Smeared in the channels of his lustful blood.

FRANKLIN

Be patient, gentle friend, and learn of me
To ease thy grief and save her chastity.   45
Entreat her fair; sweet words are fittest engines
To raze the flint walls of a woman's breast.
In any case be not too jealous,
Nor make no question of her love to thee;
But, as securely, presently take horse,   50
And lie with me at London all this term;
For women when they may will not,
But being kept back, straight grow outrageous.

ARDEN

Though this abhors from reason, yet I'll try it,
And call her forth, and presently take leave.   55
How, Alice!

Here enters ALICE

ALICE

Husband, what mean you to get up so early?
Summer nights are short, and yet you rise ere day.
Had I been wake you had not risen so soon.

ARDEN

Sweet love, thou know'st that we two, Ovid-like,   60
Have often chid the morning when it 'gan to peep,
And often wished that dark Night's purblind steeds
Would pull her by the purple mantle back

---

46 *Entreat her fair* Speak gently to her
   engines of war, but also devices, plots
47 *raze* ed. (race Qq)
50 *as securely* as if without misgivings, confidently
   presently immediately
51 *lie* lodge
   term One of the three (or four) sessions of the law courts into which the year was
   divided.
54 *abhors from* is inconsistent with, repugnant to
59 *risen* ed. (rise Qq)
60–4 *Ovid-like* Compare these lines with Ovid's Elegy XIII in Book I of the *Amores*, trans-
   lated by Christopher Marlowe.
62 *purblind* totally blind

And cast her in the ocean to her love.
But this night, sweet Alice, thou hast killed my heart;   65
I heard thee call on Mosby in thy sleep.

ALICE

'Tis like I was asleep when I named him,
For being awake he comes not in my thoughts.

ARDEN

Ay, but you started up and suddenly,
Instead of him, caught me about the neck.   70

ALICE

Instead of him? Why, who was there but you?
And where but one is how can I mistake?

FRANKLIN

Arden, leave to urge her over-far.

ARDEN

Nay, love, there is no credit in a dream.
Let it suffice I know thou lovest me well.   75

ALICE

Now I remember whereupon it came:
Had we no talk of Mosby yesternight?

FRANKLIN

Mistress Alice, I heard you name him once or twice.

ALICE

And thereof came it, and therefore blame not me.

ARDEN

I know it did, and therefore let it pass.   80
I must to London, sweet Alice, presently.

ALICE

But tell me, do you mean to stay there long?

ARDEN

No longer than till my affairs be done.

FRANKLIN

He will not stay above a month at most.

---

73 *leave* cease
74 Cf. the proverb, 'Dreams are lies' (Tilley, D587).
83 *than* ed. (there Qq). Wine quotes M. P. Jackson (*Notes and Queries*, CCVIII, 1963, p. 410), who argues for the emendation on the grounds that ' "then", which is the normal Elizabethan spelling of "than", could easily have been misread as "there", particularly under the influence of "there" in the previous line.'

ALICE

    A month? Ay me! Sweet Arden, come again   85
    Within a day or two or else I die.

ARDEN

    I cannot long be from thee, gentle Alice.
    Whilst Michael fetch our horses from the field,
    Franklin and I will down unto the quay,
    For I have certain goods there to unload.   90
    Meanwhile prepare our breakfast, gentle Alice,
    For yet ere noon we'll take horse and away.

                        Exeunt ARDEN *and* FRANKLIN

ALICE

    Ere noon he means to take horse and away!
    Sweet news is this. Oh, that some airy spirit
    Would, in the shape and likeness of a horse,   95
    Gallop with Arden 'cross the ocean
    And throw him from his back into the waves!
    Sweet Mosby is the man that hath my heart,
    And he usurps it, having nought but this—
    That I am tied to him by marriage.   100
    Love is a god, and marriage is but words,
    And therefore Mosby's title is the best.
    Tush! Whether it be or no, he shall be mine
    In spite of him, of Hymen, and of rites.

Here enters ADAM *of the Flower-de-Luce*

    And here comes Adam of the Flower-de-Luce.   105
    I hope he brings me tidings of my love.
    How now, Adam, what is the news with you?
    Be not afraid, my husband is now from home.

ADAM

    He whom you wot of, Mosby, Mistress Alice,

---

  99 *he* i.e. Arden
104 *Hymen* god of marriage
     s.d. *Flower-de-Luce* An inn, situated in Preston Street, a few minutes walk from Arden's
     house in Abbey Street. The building still stands, but is no longer used as a public house.
     It was purchased by the Faversham Society in 1972, and now houses the Fleur de Lis
     Heritage Centre. ('The prevailing form [*fleur de lis*] . . . is scarcely found in Eng. before
     the 19th c.' *O.E.D.*)
109 *wot* know

Is come to town, and sends you word by me   110
In any case you may not visit him.

ALICE

Not visit him?

ADAM

No, nor take no knowledge of his being here.

ALICE

But tell me, is he angry or displeased?

ADAM

Should seem so, for he is wondrous sad.   115

ALICE

Were he as mad as raving Hercules
I'll see him. Ay, and were thy house of force,
These hands of mine should raze it to the ground
Unless that thou wouldst bring me to my love.

ADAM

Nay, and you be so impatient, I'll be gone.   120

ALICE

Stay, Adam, stay; thou wert wont to be my friend.
Ask Mosby how I have incurred his wrath;
Bear him from me these pair of silver dice
With which we played for kisses many a time,
And when I lost I won, and so did he—   125
Such winning and such losing Jove send me!
And bid him, if his love do not decline,
To come this morning but along my door,
And as a stranger but salute me there.
This may he do without suspect or fear.   130

ADAM

I'll tell him what you say, and so farewell.   *Exit* ADAM

ALICE

Do, and one day I'll make amends for all.

---

116 Hercules was sent a shirt by his wife, Deianira, which she had woven and then soaked in
    the blood of the centaur, Nessus (whom Hercules had killed), believing that it would
    work as a charm to restore her unfaithful husband's love to her. In fact, the blood was
    poisoned, and as soon as Hercules put on the shirt he was driven raving mad by the
    pain and killed himself.
117 *of force* fortified
118 *raze* Q3 (race Q1–2)
120 *and* if
128 *To come* Q2–3 (Come Q1)

8

I know he loves me well but dares not come
Because my husband is so jealous,
And these my narrow-prying neighbours blab,   135
Hinder our meetings when we would confer.
But, if I live, that block shall be removed,
And Mosby, thou that comes to me by stealth,
Shalt neither fear the biting speech of men
Nor Arden's looks. As surely shall he die   140
As I abhor him and love only thee.

Here enters MICHAEL

How now, Michael, whither are you going?
MICHAEL
To fetch my master's nag. I hope you'll think on me.
ALICE
Ay, but Michael, see you keep your oath,
And be as secret as you are resolute.   145
MICHAEL
I'll see he shall not live above a week.
ALICE
On that condition, Michael, here is my hand:
None shall have Mosby's sister but thyself.
MICHAEL
I understand the painter here hard by
Hath made report that he and Sue is sure.   150
ALICE
There's no such matter, Michael; believe it not.
MICHAEL
But he hath sent a dagger sticking in a heart,

---

135 *narrow-prying* Q2–3 (marrow-prying Q1). As Wine notes, Q1's 'marrow-prying' is
      striking metaphorically and may be the correct reading. A similar expression is used in
      Soliman and Perseda, V.ii, 14 ('Such is the force of marrow burning loue') and in *Venus
      and Adonis*, 1. 741 ('the marrow-eating sickness'), though in both those cases it clearly
      refers to the contemporary belief that the marrow of the bones is a sexual provocative.
      Q2's reading compares with *The Taming of the Shrew*, III.ii, 142 ('The narrow-prying
      father, Minola').
137 *block* 1. obstruction 2. hard-hearted person
149 *hard by* near by
150 *sure* betrothed

9

With a verse or two stolen from a painted cloth,
The which I hear the wench keeps in her chest.
Well, let her keep it! I shall find a fellow   155
That can both write and read and make rhyme too,
And if I do—well, I say no more.
I'll send from London such a taunting letter
As she shall eat the heart he sent with salt,
And fling the dagger at the painter's head.   160

ALICE
What needs all this? I say that Susan's thine.

MICHAEL
Why then, I say that I will kill my master,
Or anything that you will have me do.

ALICE
But, Michael, see you do it cunningly.

MICHAEL
Why, say I should be took, I'll ne'er confess   165
That you know anything; and Susan, being a maid,
May beg me from the gallows of the shrieve.

ALICE
Trust not to that, Michael.

MICHAEL
You cannot tell me, I have seen it, I.
But, mistress, tell her whether I live or die   170
I'll make her more worth than twenty painters can,
For I will rid mine elder brother away,
And then the farm of Bolton is mine own.

---

153 *painted cloth* as opposed to woven cloth, and therefore a cheap substitute for tapestry.
    The design frequently incorporated verses and mottoes. (See Glynne Wickham, *Early*
    English Stages, Volume Two 1576 to 1660, Part I, 1963, p. 317, for their use as draperies
    in the playhouses.)
159 *As* That
    she ed. (not in Qq)
167 *shrieve* sheriff
166–7 It was a common belief that a virgin could save a man from being hanged by offering
    to marry him.
171 *worth* wealthy
172 *rid . . . away* i.e. kill
173 *Bolton* probably Boughton-under-Blean, a village in Kent, a few miles west of
    Canterbury.

Who would not venture upon house and land,
When he may have it for a right-down blow? 175

Here enters MOSBY

ALICE
Yonder comes Mosby. Michael, get thee gone,
And let not him nor any know thy drifts.

Exit MICHAEL

Mosby, my love!
MOSBY
Away, I say, and talk not to me now.
ALICE
A word or two, sweetheart, and then I will. 180
'Tis yet but early days; thou needest not fear.
MOSBY
Where is your husband?
ALICE
'Tis now high water, and he is at the quay.
MOSBY
There let him be; henceforward know me not.
ALICE
Is this the end of all thy solemn oaths? 185
Is this the fruit thy reconcilement buds?
Have I for this given thee so many favours,
Incurred my husband's hate, and—out, alas!—
Made shipwreck of mine honour for thy sake?
And dost thou say 'henceforward know me not'? 190
Remember when I locked thee in my closet,
What were thy words and mine? Did we not both
Decree to murder Arden in the night?
The heavens can witness, and the world can tell,
Before I saw that falsehood look of thine, 195

175 *right-down* downright
177 *drifts* schemes, plots
181 *early days* early in the day
184 Mosby's decision to reject Alice might, in performance, be underlined by his returning the silver dice, which Alice then returns to him (11. 215–6 below) as a sign of reconciliation. Presumably, it should be these same dice with which Mosby and Arden play in Scene XIV.
191 *closet* private room

'Fore I was tangled with thy 'ticing speech,
Arden to me was dearer than my soul—
And shall be still. Base peasant, get thee gone,
And boast not of thy conquest over me,
Gotten by witchcraft and mere sorcery.   200
For what hast thou to countenance my love,
Being descended of a noble house,
And matched already with a gentleman
Whose servant thou may'st be? And so farewell.

MOSBY

Ungentle and unkind, Alice; now I see   205
That which I ever feared and find too true:
A woman's love is as the lightning flame
Which even in bursting forth consumes itself.
To try thy constancy have I been strange.
Would I had never tried, but lived in hope.   210

ALICE

What needs thou try me whom thou never found false?

MOSBY

Yet pardon me, for love is jealous.

ALICE

So lists the sailor to the mermaid's song;
So looks the traveller to the basilisk.
I am content for to be reconciled,   215
And that I know will be mine overthrow.

MOSBY

Thine overthrow? First let the world dissolve!

ALICE

Nay, Mosby, let me still enjoy thy love,
And happen what will, I am resolute.
My saving husband hoards up bags of gold   220

---

196 *tangled* entangled
200 *mere* sheer, downright
201 *countenance* be in keeping with
209 *strange* distant, stand-offish
213 The mermaid, often equated in mythology with the Siren, lured sailors to destruction with her enchanting and seductive singing.
214 *the basilisk* was a fabulous reptile, hatched by a serpent from a cock's egg, whose look alone was fatal.
218 *still* always

To make our children rich, and now is he
Gone to unload the goods that shall be thine,
And he and Franklin will to London straight.

MOSBY

To London, Alice? If thou'lt be ruled by me,
We'll make him sure enough for coming there.   225

ALICE

Ah, would we could!

MOSBY

I happened on a painter yesternight,
The only cunning man of Christendom,
For he can temper poison with his oil
That whoso looks upon the work he draws   230
Shall, with the beams that issue from his sight,
Suck venom to his breast and slay himself.
Sweet Alice, he shall draw thy counterfeit,
That Arden may by gazing on it perish.

ALICE

Ay, but Mosby, that is dangerous,   235
For thou, or I, or any other else,
Coming into the chamber where it hangs, may die.

MOSBY

Ay, but we'll have it covered with a cloth
And hung up in the study for himself.

ALICE

It may not be, for when the picture's drawn,   240
Arden, I know, will come and show it me.

MOSBY

Fear not; we'll have that shall serve the turn.

---

221 *our children* No children appear in the play, but according to Holinshed, 'After supper, mistres Arden caused hir daughter to plaie on the virginals', and he later refers to 'one of mistres Ardens owne daughters.' Here, however, I think Alice is enjoying the prospect of the children she and Mosby will have being made rich by the efforts of the unsuspecting Arden.

223 *straight* straightaway

225 *for* to prevent (him) from (*O.E.D.*, 23. † d.). (See XIV.228.)

228 *only* most

   cunning possessing skill in magic

229 *temper* mix

231 It was a contemporary theory that the eyes sent out beams to the object sighted.

233 *counterfeit* portrait, likeness

This is the painter's house; I'll call him forth.

ALICE

But, Mosby, I'll have no such picture, I.

MOSBY

I pray thee leave it to my discretion.   245
How, Clarke!

Here enters CLARKE

Oh, you are an honest man of your word; you served me well.

CLARKE

Why sir, I'll do it for you at any time,
Provided, as you have given your word,
I may have Susan Mosby to my wife.   250
For as sharp-witted poets, whose sweet verse
Make heavenly gods break off their nectar draughts
And lay their ears down to the lowly earth,
Use humble promise to their sacred Muse,
So we that are the poets' favourites   255
Must have a love. Ay, love is the painter's Muse,
That makes him frame a speaking countenance,
A weeping eye that witnesses heart's grief.
Then tell me, Master Mosby, shall I have her?

ALICE

'Tis pity but he should; he'll use her well.   260

MOSBY

Clarke, here's my hand; my sister shall be thine.

CLARKE

Then, brother, to requite this courtesy,
You shall command my life, my skill, and all.

ALICE

Ah, that thou could'st be secret!

MOSBY

Fear him not. Leave; I have talked sufficient.   265

---

243 *the painter's house* probably referring to one of the doors at the rear of the stage
246 *Clarke* The name is the playwright's invention: the Faversham Wardmote Book identi-
fies him as William Blackborne.
251–6 'Just as poets need a Muse to inspire their imaginations to produce their finest work
    . . . so painters need Love to inspire them to theirs.'
257 *frame* fashion
260 *but* unless   *use* treat

CLARKE

> You know not me that ask such questions.
> Let it suffice I know you love him well,
> And fain would have your husband made away;
> Wherein, trust me, you show a noble mind,
> That rather than you'll live with him you hate,   270
> You'll venture life and die with him you love.
> The like will I do for my Susan's sake.

ALICE

> Yet nothing could enforce me to the deed
> But Mosby's love. Might I without control
> Enjoy thee still, then Arden should not die;   275
> But seeing I cannot, therefore let him die.

MOSBY

> Enough, sweet Alice; thy kind words makes me melt.
> [*To* CLARKE] Your trick of poisoned pictures we dislike;
> Some other poison would do better far.

ALICE

> Ay, such as might be put into his broth,   280
> And yet in taste not to be found at all.

CLARKE

> I know your mind, and here I have it for you.
> Put but a dram of this into his drink,
> Or any kind of broth that he shall eat,
> And he shall die within an hour after.   285

ALICE

> As I am a gentlewoman, Clarke, next day
> Thou and Susan shall be married.

MOSBY

> And I'll make her dowry more than I'll talk of, Clarke.

CLARKE

> Yonder's your husband. Mosby, I'll be gone.   *Exit* CLARKE

268 *fain* willingly, gladly

274 *control* restraint

289 s.d. *Exit* CLARKE—after l. 291 in Qq. Wine adopts Sturgess' suggestion that Michael should enter with Arden and Franklin at this point, on the grounds that Arden addresses him at l. 363, and that Qq indicate he leaves with Arden and Franklin at l. 416. Michael has not been at the quay with Arden and Franklin, however, and an entrance for him at l. 289 means he remains on stage for over 70 lines before he has anything specific to do, while during that time Arden speaks more freely than would seem likely in the presence of his servant. It is neater if Michael enters with Alice at l. 359, possibly carrying the

Here enters ARDEN *and* FRANKLIN

ALICE

    In good time. See where my husband comes,   290
    Master Mosby. Ask him the question yourself.

MOSBY

    Master Arden, being at London yesternight,
    The Abbey lands whereof you are now possessed
    Were offered me on some occasion
    By Greene, one of Sir Antony Ager's men.   295
    I pray you, sir, tell me, are not the lands yours?
    Hath any other interest herein?

ARDEN

    Mosby, that question we'll decide anon.
    Alice, make ready my breakfast; I must hence.

                                   Exit ALICE

    As for the lands, Mosby, they are mine   300
    By letters patents from his majesty.
    But I must have a mandate for my wife;
    They say you seek to rob me of her love.
    Villain, what makes thou in her company?
    She's no companion for so base a groom.   305

MOSBY

    Arden, I thought not on her, I came to thee;
    But rather than I pocket up this wrong—

FRANKLIN

    What will you do, sir?

stools on which Arden and Mosby sit. He could then either (a) exit after l. 363 and
enter again shortly afterwards (possibly on l. 382 while Franklin is giving Arden the
mithridate) which may prompt Franklin's line at 384, or (b) since the pace of this section
of the scene means an entrance might distract attention from the main focus and lessen
the tension, Michael's intended exit at l. 363 could be delayed by Arden's sudden distress,
and he could remain on stage until exiting with Arden and Franklin at l. 416.

290 *In good time* spoken to the departing Clarke.
290–1 *See . . . yourself* Alice speaks these lines for Arden to hear, in order to allay his
    suspicions at finding her with Mosby. Mosby understands immediately, and responds
    accordingly.
294 *occasion* pretext
295 *Sir Anthony Ager* in reality, Sir Anthony Aucher, a knight of Hautsbourne in Kent.
302 *mandate* deed of ownership
305 *groom* serving man (cf. I.25–30)
307 *pocket up* accept without showing resentment, 'swallow'

MOSBY

> Revenge it on the proudest of you both.

Then ARDEN *draws forth* MOSBY'S *sword*

ARDEN

> So, sirrah, you may not wear a sword.   310
> The statute makes against artificers,
> I warrant that I do. Now use your bodkin,
> Your Spanish needle, and your pressing iron,
> For this shall go with me. And mark my words,
> You goodman botcher, 'tis to you I speak: 315
> The next time that I take thee near my house,
> Instead of legs I'll make thee crawl on stumps.

MOSBY

> Ah, Master Arden, you have injured me;
> I do appeal to God and to the world.

FRANKLIN

> Why, canst thou deny wert a botcher once?   320

MOSBY

> Measure me what I am, not what I was.

ARDEN

> Why, what art thou now but a velvet drudge,
> A cheating steward, and base-minded peasant?

MOSBY

> Arden, now thou hast belched and vomited
> The rancorous venom of thy mis-swoll'n heart,   325
> Hear me but speak. As I intend to live
> With God and His elected saints in heaven,

---

310 *sirrah* 'A term of address . . . expressing contempt, reprimand, or assumption of authority on the part of the speaker' (*O.E.D.*).

311 *statute* passed under Edward III, forbidding anyone under the rank of gentleman from
wearing a sword.
makes decrees
artificers craftsmen (though *O.E.D.* † 6., notes that the word also had the contemporary
meaning of 'a trickster').

312 *I . . . do* I have warrant for what I do.

313 *Spanish needle* an embroidery needle, used for fine 'Spanish work', or 'Black work',
embroidery in black silk which was 'in the height of fashion between 1570–90
(M. Channing Linthicum, *Costume in Elizabethan Drama*, Oxford, 1936, pp. 149–50). In
view of Arden's charge that Mosby is only a *botcher*, this jibe is carefully aimed.

315 *goodman* prefixed (sometimes with ironical intention) to the names of those beneath
the rank of gentleman.

322 *velvet drudge* menial in velvet livery

I never meant more to solicit her;
And that she knows, and all the world shall see.
I loved her once—sweet Arden, pardon me.   330
I could not choose, her beauty fired my heart.
But time hath quenched these over-raging coals,
And, Arden, though I now frequent thy house,
'Tis for my sister's sake, her waiting-maid,
And not for hers. Mayest thou enjoy her long;   335
Hell-fire and wrathful vengeance light on me
If I dishonour her or injure thee.

ARDEN
Mosby, with these thy protestations
The deadly hatred of my heart is appeased,
And thou and I'll be friends if this prove true.   340
As for the base terms I gave thee late,
Forget them, Mosby; I had cause to speak
When all the knights and gentlemen of Kent
Make common table-talk of her and thee.

MOSBY
Who lives that is not touched with slanderous tongues?   345

FRANKLIN
Then, Mosby, to eschew the speech of men,
Upon whose general bruit all honour hangs,
Forbear his house.

ARDEN
Forbear it! Nay, rather frequent it more.
The world shall see that I distrust her not.   350
To warn him on the sudden from my house
Were to confirm the rumour that is grown.

MOSBY
By my faith, sir, you say true,
And therefore will I sojourn here awhile
Until our enemies have talked their fill;   355
And then, I hope, they'll cease and at last confess
How causeless they have injured her and me.

341 *late* just now
347 *bruit* report, opinion
353 *my faith* ed. (faith my Qq)

ARDEN

And I will lie at London all this term
To let them see how light I weigh their words.

Here enters ALICE [*and* MICHAEL]

ALICE

Husband, sit down; your breakfast will be cold.   360
ARDEN

Come, Master Mosby, will you sit with us?
MOSBY

I cannot eat, but I'll sit for company.
ARDEN

Sirrah Michael, see our horse be ready.

[*Exit* MICHAEL]
ALICE

Husband, why pause ye? Why eat you not?
ARDEN

I am not well; there's something in this broth   365
That is not wholesome. Didst thou make it, Alice?
ALICE

I did, and that's the cause it likes not you.
Then she throws down the broth on the ground
There's nothing that I do can please your taste.
You were best to say I would have poisoned you.
I cannot speak or cast aside my eye,   370
But he imagines I have stepped awry.
Here's he that you cast in my teeth so oft;
Now will I be convinced or purge myself.
I charge thee speak to this mistrustful man,
Thou that wouldst see me hang, thou, Mosby, thou.   375
What favour hast thou had more than a kiss
At coming or departing from the town?
MOSBY

You wrong yourself and me to cast these doubts;
Your loving husband is not jealous.
ARDEN

Why, gentle Mistress Alice, cannot I be ill   380

367 *likes not you* displeases you, offends you
373 *convinced* proved guilty

But you'll accuse yourself?
Franklin, thou has a box of mithridate;

[*Enter* MICHAEL]

I'll take a little to prevent the worst.

FRANKLIN

Do so, and let us presently take horse.
My life for yours, ye shall do well enough.   385

ALICE

Give me a spoon; I'll eat of it myself.
Would it were full of poison to the brim!
Then should my cares and troubles have an end.
Was ever silly woman so tormented?

ARDEN

Be patient, sweet love; I mistrust not thee.   390

ALICE

God will revenge it, Arden, if thou dost,
For never woman loved her husband better
Than I do thee.

ARDEN

I know it, sweet Alice; cease to complain,
Lest that in tears I answer thee again.   395

FRANKLIN

Come, leave this dallying, and let us away.

ALICE

Forbear to wound me with that bitter word.
Arden shall go to London in my arms.

ARDEN

Loth am I to depart, yet I must go.

ALICE

Wilt thou to London, then, and leave me here?   400
Ah, if thou love me, gentle Arden, stay.
Yet if thy business be of great import,
Go if thou wilt; I'll bear it as I may.

---

382 *mithridate* a universal antidote, 'so called from Mithridates VI, king of Pontus (died
      c. 63 B.C.), who was said to have rendered himself proof against poisons by the constant
      use of antidotes' (*O.E.D.*).
389 *silly* helpless, defenceless

But write from London to me every week,
Nay, every day, and stay no longer there   405
Than thou must needs, lest that I die for sorrow.

ARDEN

I'll write unto thee every other tide,
And so farewell, sweet Alice, till we meet next.

ALICE

Farewell, husband, seeing you'll have it so.
And, Master Franklin, seeing you take him hence,   410
In hope you'll hasten him home I'll give you this.

                              And then she kisseth him

FRANKLIN

And if he stay the fault shall not be mine.
Mosby, farewell, and see you keep your oath.

MOSBY

I hope he is not jealous of me now.

ARDEN

No, Mosby, no; hereafter think of me   415
As of your dearest friend. And so farewell.

              Exeunt ARDEN, FRANKLIN *and* MICHAEL

ALICE

I am glad he is gone; he was about to stay,
But did you mark me then how I brake off?

MOSBY

Ay, Alice, and it was cunningly performed.
But what a villain is this painter Clarke!   420

ALICE

Was it not a goodly poison that he gave!
Why, he's as well now as he was before.
It should have been some fine confection
That might have given the broth some dainty taste.
This powder was too gross and populous.   425

MOSBY

But had he eaten but three spoonfuls more,
Then had he died and our love continued.

ALICE

Why, so it shall, Mosby, albeit he live.

---

423 *confection* 1. mixture, compound 2. deadly poison
425 *gross and populous* indigestible and perceptible (Wine)

MOSBY
  It is unpossible, for I have sworn
  Never hereafter to solicit thee   430
  Or, whilst he lives, once more importune thee.
ALICE
  Thou shalt not need; I will importune thee.
  What, shall an oath make thee forsake my love?
  As if I have not sworn as much myself,
  And given my hand unto him in the church!   435
  Tush, Mosby. Oaths are words, and words is wind,
  And wind is mutable. Then I conclude
  'Tis childishness to stand upon an oath.
MOSBY
  Well proved, Mistress Alice; yet, by your leave,
  I'll keep mine unbroken whilst he lives.   440
ALICE
  Ay, do, and spare not. His time is but short,
  For if thou beest as resolute as I,
  We'll have him murdered as he walks the streets.
  In London many alehouse ruffians keep,
  Which, as I hear, will murder men for gold.   445
  They shall be soundly fee'd to pay him home.

Here enters GREENE

MOSBY
  Alice, what's he that comes yonder? Knowest thou him?
ALICE
  Mosby, be gone. I hope 'tis one that comes
  To put in practice our intended drifts.
                                                      Exit MOSBY

GREENE
  Mistress Arden, you are well met.   450
  I am sorry that your husband is from home
  Whenas my purposed journey was to him.
  Yet all my labour is not spent in vain,
  For I suppose that you can full discourse

444 *keep* lodge, live
446 *to pay him home* i.e. to kill him
454 *full discourse* fully explain

And flat resolve me of the thing I seek.   455
ALICE
What is it, Master Greene? If that I may
Or can with safety, I will answer you.
GREENE
I heard your husband hath the grant of late,
Confirmed by letters patents from the king,
Of all of the lands of the Abbey of Faversham,   460
Generally intitled, so that all former grants
Are cut off, whereof I myself had one;
But now my interest by that is void.
This is all, Mistress Arden; is it true nor no?
ALICE
True, Master Greene; the lands are his in state,   465
And whatsoever leases were before
Are void for term of Master Arden's life.
He hath the grant under the Chancery seal.
GREENE
Pardon me, Mistress Arden; I must speak
For I am touched. Your husband doth me wrong   470
To wring me from the little land I have.
My living is my life; only that
Resteth remainder of my portion.
Desire of wealth is endless in his mind,
And he is greedy-gaping still for gain.   475
Nor cares he though young gentlemen do beg,
So he may scrape and hoard up in his pouch.
But seeing he hath taken my lands, I'll value life
As careless as he is careful for to get;
And tell him this from me: I'll be revenged,   480

455 *flat resolve* make completely clear to
461 *Generally intitled* Deeded without any exceptions
465 *in state* by law (see XIII.19–20)
467 *term* the duration
468 The Court of the Lord Chancellor was the highest in the land, next to the House of
      Lords.
470 *touched* affected, disturbed
472 *living* property, land
473 *only . . . portion* only my land remains of what I inherited
475 *still* always
477 *So* So long as

And so as he shall wish the Abbey lands
Had rested still within their former state.

ALICE

Alas, poor gentleman, I pity you,
And woe is me that any man should want.
God knows, 'tis not my fault. But wonder not   485
Though he be hard to others when to me
Ah, Master Greene, God knows how I am used!

GREENE

Why, Mistress Arden, can the crabbed churl
Use you unkindly? Respects he not your birth,
Your honourable friends, nor what you brought?   490
Why, all Kent knows your parentage and what you are.

ALICE

Ah, Master Greene, be it spoken in secret here,
I never live good day with him alone.
When he is at home, then have I froward looks,
Hard words, and blows to mend the match withal.   495
And though I might content as good a man,
Yet doth he keep in every corner trulls;
And weary with his trugs at home,
Then rides he straight to London; there, forsooth,
He revels it among such filthy ones   500
As counsels him to make away his wife.
Thus live I daily in continual fear,
In sorrow, so despairing of redress
As every day I wish with hearty prayer
That he or I were taken forth the world.   505

GREENE

Now trust me, Mistress Alice, it grieveth me
So fair a creature should be so abused.
Why, who would have thought the civil sir so sullen?
He looks so smoothly. Now, fie upon him, churl!
And if he live a day he lives too long.   510

488 *crabbed* ill-natured
490 *what you brought* i.e. your dowry
494 *froward* bad tempered
495 *mend the match* make up the marriage bargain (Sturgess)
497 *trulls, trugs* whores, prostitutes
509 *smoothly* courteous

But frolic, woman; I shall be the man
Shall set you free from all this discontent.
And if the churl deny my interest,
And will not yield my lease into my hand,
I'll pay him home, whatever hap to me.   515

ALICE

But speak you as you think?

GREENE

Ay, God's my witness, I mean plain dealing,
For I had rather die than lose my land.

ALICE

Then, Master Greene, be counselled by me:
Endanger not yourself for such a churl,   520
But hire some cutter for to cut him short;
And here's ten pound to wager them withal.
When he is dead you shall have twenty more,
And the lands whereof my husband is possessed
Shall be intitled as they were before.   525

GREENE

Will you keep promise with me?

ALICE

Or count me false and perjured whilst I live.

GREENE

Then here's my hand, I'll have him so dispatched.
I'll up to London straight; I'll thither post,
And never rest till I have compassed it.   530
Till then farewell.

ALICE

Good fortune follow all your forward thoughts.

                                            Exit GREENE

And whosoever doth attempt the deed
A happy hand I wish, and so farewell.
All this goes well. Mosby, I long for thee   535
To let thee know all that I have contrived.

511 *frolic* cheer up
513 *interest* legal right to property
521 *cutter* cut-throat
522 *wager* pay
529 *post* travel without delay
532 *forward* eager

Here enters MOSBY *and* CLARKE

MOSBY
How now, Alice, what's the news?

ALICE
Such as will content thee well, sweetheart.

MOSBY
Well, let them pass awhile, and tell me, Alice,
How have you dealt and tempered with my sister?   540
What, will she have my neighbour Clarke or no?

ALICE
What, Master Mosby! Let him woo himself.
Think you that maids look not for fair words?
Go to her, Clarke, she's all alone within.
Michael, my man, is clean out of her books.   545

CLARKE
I thank you, Mistress Arden, I will in,
And if fair Susan and I can make a gree,
You shall command me to the uttermost,
As far as either goods or life may stretch.   *Exit* CLARKE

MOSBY
Now, Alice, let's hear thy news.   550

ALICE
They be so good that I must laugh for joy
Before I can begin to tell my tale.

MOSBY
Let's hear them, that I may laugh for company.

ALICE
This morning, Master Greene—Dick Greene, I mean,
From whom my husband had the Abbey land   555
Came hither railing for to know the truth,
Whether my husband had the lands by grant.
I told him all, whereat he stormed amain
And swore he would cry quittance with the churl
And, if he did deny his interest,   560

---

539   *them* i.e. the news
540   *tempered with* persuaded
547   *make a gree* come to terms
558   *amain* vehemently, violently
559   *cry quittance with* get even with

26

Stab him, whatsoever did befall himself.
Whenas I saw his choler thus to rise,
I whetted on the gentleman with words,
And, to conclude, Mosby, at last we grew
To composition for my husband's death.   565
I gave him ten pound to hire knaves
By some device to make away the churl.
When he is dead he should have twenty more
And repossess his former lands again.
On this we 'greed, and he is ridden straight   570
To London to bring his death about.

MOSBY
But call you this good news?

ALICE
Ay, sweetheart, be they not?

MOSBY
'Twere cheerful news to hear the churl were dead,
But trust me, Alice, I take it passing ill   575
You would be so forgetful of our state
To make recount of it to every groom.
What! to acquaint each stranger with our drifts,
Chiefly in case of murder! Why, 'tis the way
To make it open unto Arden's self,   580
And bring thyself and me to ruin both.
Forewarned, forearmed; who threats his enemy
Lends him a sword to guard himself withal.

ALICE
I did it for the best.

MOSBY
Well, seeing 'tis done, cheerly let it pass.   585
You know this Greene; is he not religious?
A man, I guess, of great devotion?

ALICE
He is.

MOSBY
Then, sweet Alice, let it pass. I have a drift
Will quiet all, whatever is amiss.   590

563 *whetted on* incited
565 *composition* agreement (for payment)
575 *passing* extremely

Here enters CLARKE *and* SUSAN

ALICE

How now, Clarke, have you found me false?
Did I not plead the matter hard for you?

CLARKE

You did.

MOSBY

And what? Will't be a match?

CLARKE

A match, i'faith, sir. Ay, the day is mine. 595
The painter lays his colours to the life,
His pencil draws no shadows in his love;
Susan is mine.

ALICE

You make her blush.

MOSBY

What, sister, is it Clarke must be the man? 600

SUSAN

It resteth in your grant. Some words are passed,
And haply we be grown unto a match
If you be willing that it shall be so.

MOSBY

Ah, Master Clarke, it resteth at my grant;
You see my sister's yet at my dispose. 605
But, so you'll grant me one thing I shall ask,
I am content my sister shall be yours.

CLARKE

What is it, Master Mosby?

MOSBY

I do remember once in secret talk
You told me how you could compound by art 610
A crucifix impoisoned,
That whoso look upon it should wax blind,
And with the scent be stifled, that ere long
He should die poisoned that did view it well.
I would have you make me such a crucifix, 615
And then I'll grant my sister shall be yours.

596–7 'The painter reproduces life faithfully, and, in this case, his pencil need draw no shadows in his love.'
602 *haply* perhaps

CLARKE

    Though I am loth, because it toucheth life,
    Yet rather or I'll leave sweet Susan's love
    I'll do it, and with all the haste I may.
    But for whom is it?   620

ALICE

    Leave that to us. Why, Clarke, is it possible
    That you should paint and draw it out yourself,
    The colours being baleful and impoisoned,
    And no ways prejudice yourself withal?

MOSBY

    Well questioned, Alice. Clarke, how answer you that?   625

CLARKE

    Very easily. I'll tell you straight
    How I do work of these impoisoned drugs:
    I fasten on my spectacles so close
    As nothing can any way offend my sight;
    Then, as I put a leaf within my nose,   630
    So put I rhubarb to avoid the smell,
    And softly as another work I paint.

MOSBY

    'Tis very well, but against when shall I have it?

CLARKE

    Within this ten days.

MOSBY

    'Twill serve the turn.   635
    Now, Alice, let's in and see what cheer you keep.

                                   [*Exit* CLARKE]

    I hope now Master Arden is from home,
    You'll give me leave to play your husband's part.

ALICE

    Mosby, you know who's master of my heart;
    He well may be the master of the house.

                                    Exeunt

---

618 *or* than
623 *baleful* noxious, harmful
624 *prejudice* endanger
629 *offend* damage
631 *rhubarb* believed to have medicinal properties, and used as a purgative drug.
632 *softly as another* as easily as with any other

SCENE II

Here enters GREENE *and* BRADSHAW

BRADSHAW
  See you them that comes yonder, Master Greene?
GREENE
  Ay, very well. Do you know them?

Here enters BLACK WILL *and* SHAKEBAG

BRADSHAW
  The one I know not, but he seems a knave,
  Chiefly for bearing the other company;
  For such a slave, so vile a rogue as he,   5
  Lives not again upon the earth.
  Black Will is his name. I tell you, Master Greene,
  At Boulogne he and I were fellow soldiers,
  Where he played such pranks
  As all the camp feared him for his villainy.   10
  I warrant you he bears so bad a mind
  That for a crown he'll murder any man.
GREENE [*Aside*]
  The fitter is he for my purpose, marry!
BLACK WILL
  How now, fellow Bradshaw! Whither away so early?
BRADSHAW
  Oh, Will, times are changed; no fellows now,   15
  Though we were once together in the field;
  Yet thy friend to do thee any good I can.
BLACK WILL
  Why, Bradshaw, was not thou and I fellow soldiers at Boulogne,
  where I was a corporal and thou but a base mercenary groom?
  'No fellows now' because you are a goldsmith and have a little   20
  plate in your shop? You were glad to call me 'fellow Will' and,

---

8 *Boulogne* French port on the English Channel. It was captured by Henry VIII in 1544,
  and restored to France by Edward VI in 1550.
11 *warrant* assure
13 *marry!* an oath derived from the name of the Virgin Mary.

with a curtsey to the earth, 'one snatch, good corporal', when I
stole the half ox from John the victualler, and domineered with
it amongst good fellows in one night.

BRADSHAW

Ay, Will, those days are past with me.   25

BLACK WILL

Ay, but they be not past with me, for I keep that same
honourable mind still. Good neighbour Bradshaw, you are too
proud to be my fellow, but were it not that I see more company
coming down the hill, I would be fellows with you once more,
and share crowns with you too. But let that pass, and tell me   30
whither you go.

BRADSHAW

To London, Will, about a piece of service
Wherein haply thou may'st pleasure me.

BLACK WILL

What is it?

BRADSHAW

Of late, Lord Cheiny lost some plate,   35
Which one did bring and sold it at my shop,
Saying he served Sir Antony Cooke.
A search was made, the plate was found with me,
And I am bound to answer at the 'size.
Now Lord Cheiny solemnly vows,   40
If law will serve him, he'll hang me for his plate.
Now I am going to London upon hope

---

22 *curtsey* ed. (cursy Qq) bow
   snatch morsel
23 *domineered* revelled
30 *share crowns with you* i.e. rob you
35–9 *Of late ... next 'size* It has been suggested that the episode has local relevance and
   indicates either that the author was from Kent, or that the lines were added to the prompt
   copy by the actors who were touring the play in that county.
   It serves, however, a number of important dramatic functions; firstly, it allows Greene
   time to compose the letter to Alice (see VIII.153–60, and XVIII.2–7); secondly, it
   skilfully establishes the new characters of Black Will and Shakebag; and thirdly, if, as
   seems likely (the striking physical description Bradshaw gives of Fitten would scarcely
   seem to require the further details of his apparel), Black Will is deliberately spinning out
   the time before he reveals Fitten's name, making Bradshaw pay up while he does so, it
   establishes Bradshaw as an innocent man used by others, a role he plays with fatal results.
37 *Sir Anthony Cooke* (1504–76) tutor to Edward VI.
39 *'size* assize (usually in plural)

To find the fellow. Now, Will, I know
Thou art acquainted with such companions.

BLACK WILL

What manner of man was he?   45

BRADSHAW

A lean-faced, writhen knave,
Hawk-nosed and very hollow-eyed,
With mighty furrows in his stormy brows,
Long hair down his shoulders curled;
His chin was bare, but on his upper lip   50
A mutchado, which he wound about his ear.

BLACK WILL

What apparel had he?

BRADSHAW

A watchet satin doublet all to-torn
(The inner side did bear the greater show),
A pair of threadbare velvet hose, seam rent,   55
A worsted stocking rent above the shoe,
A livery cloak, but all the lace was off;
'Twas bad, but yet it served to hide the plate.

BLACK WILL

Sirrah Shakebag, canst thou remember since we trolled the bowl
at Sittingburgh, where I broke the tapster's head of the Lion   60
with a cudgel-stick?

SHAKEBAG

Ay, very well, Will.

BLACK WILL

Why, it was with the money that the plate was sold for. Sirrah
Bradshaw, what wilt thou give him that can tell thee who sold
thy plate?   65

BRADSHAW

Who, I pray thee, good Will?

---

46 *writhen* cringing, twisted
51 *mutchado* moustache
53 *watchet* light blue
    all to-torn completely torn
54 *The. . . . show* more of the lining than the outside was visible
56 *worsted* ed. (wosted Q1, 3; wosten Q2)
59 *trolled the bowl* passed round the drinking cup, celebrated
60 *Sittingburgh* i.e. Sittingbourne, a town in Kent about 9 miles east of Faversham.
    tapster's head of the Lion i.e., the head of the tapster (barman) at the Lion Inn.

BLACK WILL

Why, 'twas one Jack Fitten. He's now in Newgate for stealing a
horse, and shall be arraigned the next 'size.

BRADSHAW

Why then, let Lord Cheiny seek Jack Fitten forth,
For I'll back and tell him who robbed him of his plate.   70
This cheers my heart. Master Greene, I'll leave you,
For I must to the Isle of Sheppey with speed.

GREENE

Before you go, let me entreat you
To carry this letter to Mistress Arden of Faversham
And humbly recommend me to herself.   75

BRADSHAW

That will I, Master Greene, and so farewell.
Here, Will, there's a crown for thy good news.

Exit BRADSHAW

BLACK WILL

Farewell, Bradshaw; I'll drink no water for thy sake whilst this
lasts. Now, gentleman, shall we have your company to London?

GREENE

Nay, stay, sirs,   80
A little more: I needs must use your help,
And in a matter of great consequence,
Wherein if you'll be secret and profound,
I'll give you twenty angels for your pains.

BLACK WILL

How? Twenty angels? Give my fellow George Shakebag and me   85
twenty angels, and if thou'lt have thy own father slain that thou
mayest inherit his land we'll kill him.

SHAKEBAG

Ay, thy mother, thy sister, thy brother, or all thy kin.

---

67 *Newgate* The 'chief prison of London. Those who were condemned to death were carted
   out to Tyburn for execution: the dismal procession passed by St. Sepulchre's church,
   where a nosegay was given to the condemned man' (Sugden).

68 *arraigned* indicted, charged

72 *Isle of Sheppey* 'an island in Kent, separated from the mainland by a branch of the
   Medway . . . just opposite to Faversham' (Sugden).

83 *profound* cunning

84 *angels* gold coins worth about 10 shillings. They were embossed with the device of the
   Archangel Michael slaying the dragon.

GREENE

Well, this it is: Arden of Faversham
Hath highly wronged me about the Abbey land,   90
That no revenge but death will serve the turn.
Will you two kill him? Here's the angels down,
And I will lay the platform of his death.

BLACK WILL

Plat me no platforms! Give me the money and I'll stab him as
he stands pissing against a wall, but I'll kill him.   95

SHAKEBAG

Where is he?

GREENE

He is now at London, in Aldersgate Street.

SHAKEBAG

He's dead as if he had been condemned by an Act of Parliament
if once Black Will and I swear his death.

GREENE

Here is ten pound, and when he is dead   100
Ye shall have twenty more.

BLACK WILL

My fingers itches to be at the peasant. Ah, that I might be set a
work thus through the year and that murder would grow to an
occupation that a man might without danger of law. Zounds! I
warrant I should be warden of the company. Come, let us be   105
going, and we'll bait at Rochester, where I'll give thee a gallon of
sack to handsel the match withal.

Exeunt

---

93 *lay the platform* devise the plan
97 *Aldersgate Street* ran south from Aldersgate 'to St. Martin's-le-Grand, and so into the
   west end of Cheapside . . . the town houses of the Earls of Northumberland, Westmorland,
   and Thanet, and of the Marquis of Dorchester, were in this street' (Sugden).
102 *might* i.e., might follow it
104 *Zounds!* oath derived from 'By God's wounds'.
105 *warden of the company* Black Will imagines a company dealing in murder and extortion
   (see XIV.5–27) being established as one of the legitimate Livery Companies of the City
   of London, with himself as *warden* (that is, the governor, or member of the governing
   body) of the company.
106 *bait* stop for food and rest
   Rochester 'ancient episcopal city in Kent, on the Medway, 33 miles east of London'
   (Sugden).
107 *sack* white wine, imported from Spain and the Canaries.
   handsel seal with success

SCENE III

Here enters MICHAEL

MICHAEL
I have gotten such a letter as will touch the painter, and thus it is:

Here enters ARDEN *and* FRANKLIN *and hears*
MICHAEL *read this letter*

'My duty remembered, Mistress Susan, hoping in God you be in
good health, as I, Michael, was at the making hereof. This is to
certify you that, as the turtle true, when she hath lost her mate,
sitteth alone, so I, mourning for your absence, do walk up and   5
down Paul's till one day I fell asleep and lost my master's
pantofles. Ah, Mistress Susan, abolish that paltry painter, cut
him off by the shins with a frowning look of your crabbed
countenance, and think upon Michael, who, drunk with the
dregs of your favour, will cleave as fast to your love as a plaster   10
of pitch to a galled horseback. Thus hoping you will let my
passions penetrate, or rather impetrate, mercy of your meek
hands, I end.

       Yours, Michael, or else not Michael.'

ARDEN
Why, you paltry knave!   15
Stand you here loitering, knowing my affairs,

---

4 *certify* assure
 turtle turtle dove
6 *Paul's* i.e., St Paul's Cathedral in London. The middle aisle of the Cathedral, known
 as Paul's Walk (or Duke Humphrey's Walk), was a popular meeting-place for merchants
 and businessmen, as well as being the haunt of prostitutes and pickpockets (see
 ll. 46–7)
7 *pantofles* overshoes or galoshes; presumably entrusted to Michael's care while Arden was
 inside the Cathedral doing business.
10–11 *plaster . . . horseback* 'part of a remedy suggested by Nicholas Maltby (supposed
 author) in *Remedies for diseases in Horses* (London, 1576)' (Wine).
11 *galled* sore with chafing
12 *impetrate* obtain by request, beseech

What haste my business craves to send to Kent?

FRANKLIN

'Faith, friend Michael, this is very ill,
Knowing your master hath no more but you,
And do ye slack his business for your own?   20

ARDEN

Where is the letter, sirrah? Let me see it.

Then he [MICHAEL] *gives him the letter*

See, Master Franklin, here's proper stuff:
Susan my maid, the painter, and my man,
A crew of harlots, all in love, forsooth.
Sirrah, let me hear no more of this,   25
Nor, for thy life, once write to her a word.

Here enters GREENE, [BLACK] WILL, *and* SHAKEBAG

Wilt thou be married to so base a trull?
'Tis Mosby's sister. Come I once at home
I'll rouse her from remaining in my house.
Now, Master Franklin, let us go walk in Paul's.   30
Come, but a turn or two and then away.

Exeunt [ARDEN, FRANKLIN, *and* MICHAEL]

GREENE

The first is Arden, and that's his man.
The other is Franklin, Arden's dearest friend.

BLACK WILL

Zounds, I'll kill them all three.

GREENE

Nay, sirs, touch not his man in any case;   35
But stand close and take you fittest standing,

---

17 *send* i.e. to be sent

21 Michael's letter is clearly a parody of the euphuistic style (named after John Lyly's *Euphues, The Anatomy of Wit*, 1578, and *Euphues and His England*, 1580), with its elaborate rhetorical devices and sentence structure, similes, word-play, proverbs, and fables. Here, obviously, the comic effect is achieved by the stark contrast between the form and the actual content of the letter.

24 *harlots* lewd persons of either sex

26 *Nor* ed. (Now Qq)

36 *stand close* conceal yourselves

fittest standing best position (with the sense, as it is used specifically in IX.38, of a 'stand from which to shoot game', which ties in with the hunting imagery and terminology which runs through the play.) *O.E.D.* also notes that *standing* can refer to the position occupied by a stall, or to the stall itself.

And at his coming forth speed him.
To the Nag's Head, there is this coward's haunt.
But now I'll leave you till the deed be done.　　*Exit* GREENE
SHAKEBAG
If he be not paid his own, ne'er trust Shakebag.　　　　　　　40
BLACK WILL
Sirrah Shakebag, at his coming forth I'll run him through, and
then to the Blackfriars and there take water and away.
SHAKEBAG
Why, that's the best; but see thou miss him not.
BLACK WILL
How can I miss him, when I think on the forty angels I must
have more?　　　　　　　　　　　　　　　　　　　　45

Here enters a PRENTICE

PRENTICE
'Tis very late; I were best shut up my stall, for here will be old
filching when the press comes forth of Paul's.
　　　　　　　Then lets he down his window, and it breaks
　　　　　　　　　　　　　　　　BLACK WILL'*s head*
BLACK WILL
Zounds! Draw, Shakebag, draw! I am almost killed.

37　*speed* kill, dispatch
38　*Nag's Head* 'A tavern in London, at the East corner of Cheapside and Friday Street'
　　(Sugden).
40　*paid his own* i.e. killed
42　*Blackfriars* A fashionable district of London which retained the right of sanctuary even
　　after the dissolution of the Dominican monastery in 1538.
　　take water take a boat across the Thames
46　*stall* i.e., book stall. St Paul's churchyard was a centre for selling books, and the sellers'
　　stocks were stored in the vaults of the Cathedral. The title-page of the 1592 Quarto of
　　Arden (see p. 1) indicates that its publisher, Edward White, had his business at 'the lyttle
　　North dore of Paules Church at the signe of the Gun', and the title-page itself with its
　　lurid and selective account of the play's contents would have been displayed on the front
　　of the stall to arouse the interest of potential customers.
46–7　*old filching* much pilfering
47　*press* crowd
　　s.d. A simple structure resembling a book-seller's stall, and incorporating a practical
　　window or shutter which could be 'let down' is needed here, and would probably be
　　brought on stage for this scene only.
　　breaks grazes, bruises

PRENTICE

We'll tame you, I warrant.

BLACK WILL

Zounds, I am tame enough already.   50

Here enters ARDEN, FRANKLIN, *and* MICHAEL

ARDEN

What troublesome fray or mutiny is this?

FRANKLIN

'Tis nothing but some brabbling, paltry fray,

Devised to pick men's pockets in the throng.

ARDEN

Is't nothing else? Come, Franklin, let us away.

Exeunt [ARDEN, FRANKLIN, *and* MICHAEL]

BLACK WILL

What 'mends shall I have for my broken head?   55

PRENTICE

Marry, this 'mends, that if you get you not away all the sooner,

you shall be well beaten and sent to the Counter.

Exit PRENTICE

BLACK WILL

Well, I'll be gone; but look to your signs, for I'll pull them down

all. Shakebag, my broken head grieves me not so much as by

this means Arden hath escaped.   60

Here enters GREENE

I had a glimpse of him and his companion.

GREENE

Why, sirs, Arden's as well as I; I met him and Franklin going

merrily to the ordinary. What, dare you not do it?

49 *tame* hurt
52 *brabbling* riotous, brawling
56 *'mends* cure, reparation
57 *Counter* a London prison.
59 *as* as the fact that
63 *ordinary* a tavern, or its dining room, where meals were provided at a fixed price, e.g.,
    18 pence, as at 1. 121.

BLACK WILL

Yes, sir, we dare do it; but were my consent to give again we
would not do it under ten pound more. I value every drop of   65
my blood at a French crown. I have had ten pound to steal a
dog, and we have no more here to kill a man. But that a bargain
is a bargain and so forth, you should do it yourself.

GREENE

I pray thee, how came thy head broke?

BLACK WILL

Why, thou seest it is broke, dost thou not?   70

SHAKEBAG

Standing against a stall, watching Arden's coming, a boy let
down his shop window and broke his head; whereupon arose a
brawl, and in the tumult Arden escaped us and passed by
unthought on. But forbearance is no acquittance; another time
we'll do it, I warrant thee.   75

GREENE

I pray thee, Will, make clean thy bloody brow,
And let us bethink us on some other place
Where Arden may be met with handsomely.
Remember how devoutly thou hast sworn
To kill the villain; think upon thine oath.   80

BLACK WILL

Tush, I have broken five hundred oaths!
But wouldst thou charm me to effect this deed,
Tell me of gold, my resolution's fee;
Say thou seest Mosby kneeling at my knees,
Off'ring me service for my high attempt;   85
And sweet Alice Arden, with a lap of crowns,
Comes with a lowly curtsey to the earth,
Saying 'Take this but for thy quarterage;
Such yearly tribute will I answer thee.'

---

78 *handsomely* conveniently
83 *Say thou ... of crowns* These lines (see also 11. 112–15 below), where a character
   possesses unexpected information or knowledge, or (see 1. 32 and 1. 122 in this scene)
   where there appears to be an inconsistency, may be, as Wine notes, signs of authorial
   confusion or textual corruption, but (unlike the letter in Scene VIII.156–8) they are
   unlikely to trouble an audience
88 *quarterage* quarterly payment
89 *answer* guarantee

Why, this would steel soft-mettled cowardice, 90
With which Black Will was never tainted with.
I tell thee, Greene, the forlorn traveller,
Whose lips are glued with summer's parching heat,
Ne'er longed so much to see a running brook
As I to finish Arden's tragedy. 95
Seest thou this gore that cleaveth to my face?
From hence ne'er will I wash this bloody stain
Till Arden's heart be panting in my hand.

GREENE

Why, that's well said; but what saith Shakebag?

SHAKEBAG

I cannot paint my valour out with words; 100
But give me place and opportunity,
Such mercy as the starven lioness,
When she is dry-sucked of her eager young,
Shows to the prey that next encounters her,
On Arden so much pity would I take. 105

GREENE

So should it fare with men of firm resolve.
And now, sirs, seeing this accident
Of meeting him in Paul's hath no success,
Let us bethink us on some other place
Whose earth may swallow up this Arden's blood. 110

Here enters MICHAEL

See, yonder comes his man. And wot you what?
The foolish knave is in love with Mosby's sister,
And for her sake, whose love he cannot get
Unless Mosby solicit his suit,
The villain hath sworn the slaughter of his master. 115
We'll question him, for he may stead us much.
How now, Michael, whither are you going?

MICHAEL

My master hath new supped,
And I am going to prepare his chamber.

GREENE

Where supped Master Arden? 120

116 *stead us much* give us useful information

MICHAEL

At the Nag's Head, at the eighteen pence ordinary. How now,
Master Shakebag! What, Black Will! God's dear lady, how
chance your face is so bloody?

BLACK WILL

Go to, sirrah; there is a chance in it this sauciness in you will
make you be knocked. 125

MICHAEL

Nay, and you be offended, I'll be gone.

GREENE

Stay, Michael, you may not 'scape us so.
Michael, I know you love your master well.

MICHAEL

Why, so I do; but wherefore urge you that?

GREENE

Because I think you love your mistress better. 130

MICHAEL

So think not I. But say, i'faith, what if I should?

SHAKEBAG

Come to the purpose. Michael, we hear
You have a pretty love in Faversham.

MICHAEL

Why, have I two or three, what's that to thee?

BLACK WILL

You deal too mildly with the peasant. Thus it is: 135
'Tis known to us you love Mosby's sister;
We know besides that you have ta'en your oath
To further Mosby to your mistress' bed
And kill your master for his sister's sake.
Now, sir, a poorer coward than yourself 140
Was never fostered in the coast of Kent.
How comes it then that such a knave as you
Dare swear a matter of such consequence?

GREENE

Ah, Will

124 *Go to* exclamation of protest
129 *urge* bring up
134 s.p. Q2–3 (not in Q1)
136 *known* Q2–3 (kowne Q1)

41

BLACK WILL

    Tush, give me leave, there's no more but this: 145
    Sith thou hast sworn, we dare discover all,
    And hadst thou or shouldst thou utter it,
    We have devised a complot under hand,
    Whatever shall betide to any of us,
    To send thee roundly to the devil of hell, 150
    And therefore thus: I am the very man,
    Marked in my birth-hour by the Destinies,
    To give an end to Arden's life on earth;
    Thou but a member but to whet the knife
    Whose edge must search the closet of his breast. 155
    Thy office is but to appoint the place,
    And train thy master to his tragedy;
    Mine to perform it when occasion serves.
    Then be not nice, but here devise with us
    How and what way we may conclude his death. 160

SHAKEBAG

    So shall thou purchase Mosby for thy friend,
    And by his friendship gain his sister's love.

GREENE

    So shall thy mistress be thy favourer,
    And thou disburdened of the oath thou made.

MICHAEL

    Well, gentlemen, I cannot but confess, 165
    Sith you have urged me so apparently,
    That I have vowed my master Arden's death;
    And he whose kindly love and liberal hand
    Doth challenge nought but good deserts of me
    I will deliver over to your hands. 170

146 *Sith* Since
    discover reveal
148 *complot* Q2–3 (complat Q1) plot, conspiracy
    under hand in secret
150 *roundly* promptly, directly
152 *Destinies* i.e., the three Goddesses of Fate.
154 *member* helper
157 *train* lure
159 *nice* coy, squeamish
169 *challenge* claim, deserve
    deserts of deeds in return from

This night come to his house at Aldersgate;
The doors I'll leave unlocked against you come.
No sooner shall ye enter through the latch,
Over the threshold to the inner court,
But on your left hand shall you see the stairs   175
That leads directly to my master's chamber.
There take him and dispose him as ye please.
Now it were good we parted company.
What I have promised I will perform.

BLACK WILL

Should you deceive us, 'twould go wrong with you.   180

MICHAEL

I will accomplish all I have revealed.

BLACK WILL

Come, let's go drink. Choler makes me as dry as a dog.

Exeunt [BLACK] WILL, GREENE, and SHAKEBAG

Manet MICHAEL

MICHAEL

Thus feeds the lamb securely on the down
Whilst through the thicket of an arbour brake
The hunger-bitten wolf o'erpries his haunt   185
And takes advantage to eat him up.
Ah, harmless Arden, how, how hast thou misdone
That thus thy gentle life is levelled at?
The many good turns that thou hast done to me
Now must I quittance with betraying thee.   190
I, that should take the weapon in my hand
And buckler thee from ill-intending foes,
Do lead thee with a wicked, fraudful smile,
As unsuspected to the slaughterhouse.
So have I sworn to Mosby and my mistress,   195
So have I promised to the slaughtermen;
And should I not deal currently with them,

---

172 *against you come* in anticipation of your coming
182 s.d. *Manet* remains
185 *haunt* ed. (hant Qq)
187 *harmless* innocent
188 *levelled at* aimed at, threatened
190 *quittance* repay
192 *buckler* shield, protect
197 *currently* honestly, faithfully

Their lawless rage would take revenge on me.
Tush, I will spurn at mercy for this once.
Let pity lodge where feeble women lie;   200
I am resolved, and Arden needs must die.

Exit MICHAEL

SCENE IV

Here enters ARDEN *and* FRANKLIN

ARDEN

No, Franklin, no. If fear or stormy threats,
If love of me or care of womanhood,
If fear of God or common speech of men,
Who mangle credit with their wounding words
And couch dishonour as dishonour buds,   5
Might 'join repentance in her wanton thoughts
No question then but she would turn the leaf
And sorrow for her dissolution.

4 *credit* honour, reputation
5 *couch* a difficult word, glossed differently by various editors. Warnke and Proescholdt
(*Pseudo-Shakesperian Plays*, Vol. V), suggest *spread*, comparing *couch grass*; R. Bayne
notes that if the word is used 'in its surgical sense' ('to remove a cataract' *O.E.D.* 9), the
line would mean 'Cut the bud of dishonour so that it bursts into flower.' Sturgess glosses
it as 'to embroider' (*O.E.D.* † 4b), and Wine suggests that a 'possible, but more remote,
reading might be based on *O.E.D.* 15 ('to put into words'). Brooke's suggestion (based on
O.E.D. v¹., 5 'to promote germination'), that the line 'appears to mean that scandal
mongers nourish the unripe buds of dishonour, as fast as they appear, till they sprout and
grow', has the advantage of keeping to the imagery of the speech and to a pattern of
imagery running through the whole play. According to *O.E.D.*, however, this usage refers
specifically to '*Malting*. To lay or spread (grain after steeping) on a floor to promote
germination'. Although that may be apt for a play set in Kent, a more specific, and
equally appropriate horticultural gloss (*O.E.D.* 3† c, 'to lay, set, bed (plants or slips) in
the earth'), would give the reading: 'As the buds (or shoots) of dishonour appear, so the
scandal mongers plant them in the earth (or *couch* them) to grow stronger', a reading
supported, perhaps, by l. 9, 'But she is rooted in her wickedness'.
Interestingly (in view of l. 13), the *O.E.D.* entry for *bud* (3.fig.), cites the example 'This
Hydra . . . With seven heads, budding monstrous crimes' (1591).
6 *'join* enjoin
8 *dissolution* dissolute behaviour

But she is rooted in her wickedness,
Perverse and stubborn, not to be reclaimed. 10
Good counsel is to her as rain to weeds,
And reprehension makes her vice to grow
As Hydra's head that plenished by decay.
Her faults, methink, are painted in my face
For every searching eye to overread; 15
And Mosby's name, a scandal unto mine,
Is deeply trenched in my blushing brow.
Ah, Franklin, Franklin, when I think on this,
My heart's grief rends my other powers
Worse than the conflict at the hour of death. 20

FRANKLIN
Gentle Arden, leave this sad lament.
She will amend, and so your griefs will cease;
Or else she'll die, and so your sorrows end.
If neither of these two do haply fall,
Yet let your comfort be that others bear 25
Your woes, twice doubled all, with patience.

ARDEN
My house is irksome; there I cannot rest.

FRANKLIN
Then stay with me in London; go not home.

ARDEN
Then that base Mosby doth usurp my room
And makes his triumph of my being thence. 30
At home or not at home, where'er I be,
Here, here it lies, [*Points to his heart*] ah, Franklin, here it lies
That will not out till wretched Arden dies.

Here enters MICHAEL

FRANKLIN
Forget your griefs awhile; here comes your man.

---

13 The second labour of Hercules was to kill the Lernaean Hydra, an enormous serpent with nine heads, each of which was replenished with two more when cut off; (*by decay* = ?by decapitation—Wine).
    plenished ed. (perisht Qq) replenished
17 *trenched* furrowed, carved
24 *fall* occur

ARDEN

    What o'clock is't, sirrah?

MICHAEL   Almost ten.   35

ARDEN

    See, see how runs away the weary time.

    Come, Master Franklin, shall we go to bed?

                    Exeunt ARDEN *and* MICHAEL

                            Manet FRANKLIN

FRANKLIN

    I pray you, go before; I'll follow you.

    Ah, what a hell is fretful jealousy!

    What pity-moving words, what deep-fetched sighs,   40

    What grievous groans and overlading woes

    Accompanies this gentle gentleman.

    Now will he shake his care-oppressed head,

    Then fix his sad eyes on the sullen earth,

    Ashamed to gaze upon the open world;   45

    Now will he cast his eyes up towards the heavens,

    Looking that ways for redress of wrong.

    Sometimes he seeketh to beguile his grief,

    And tells a story with his careful tongue;

    Then comes his wife's dishonour in his thoughts   50

    And in the middle cutteth off his tale,

    Pouring fresh sorrow on his weary limbs.

    So woe-begone, so inly charged with woe,

    Was never any lived and bare it so.

Here enters MICHAEL

MICHAEL

    My master would desire you come to bed.   55

FRANKLIN

    Is he himself already in his bed?

                            Exit FRANKLIN

                          Manet MICHAEL

40 *moving* Q2–3 (moning Q1)
48 *beguile* divert attention away from
49 *careful* full of care
54 *Was* i.e. There was

MICHAEL

He is and fain would have the light away.
Conflicting thoughts encamped in my breast
Awake me with the echo of their strokes;
And I, a judge to censure either side,   60
Can give to neither wished victory.
My master's kindness pleads to me for life
With just demand, and I must grant it him;
My mistress she hath forced me with an oath,
For Susan's sake the which I may not break,   65
For that is nearer than a master's love;
That grim-faced fellow, pitiless Black Will,
And Shakebag, stern in bloody stratagem
Two rougher ruffians never lived in Kent –
Have sworn my death if I infringe my vow,   70
A dreadful thing to be considered of.
Methinks I see them with their boltered hair,
Staring and grinning in thy gentle face,
And in their ruthless hands their daggers drawn,
Insulting o'er thee with a peck of oaths   75
Whilst thou, submissive, pleading for relief,
Art mangled by their ireful instruments.
Methinks I hear them ask where Michael is,
And pitiless Black Will cries 'Stab the slave!
The peasant will detect the tragedy.'   80
The wrinkles in his foul, death-threat'ning face
Gapes open wide, like graves to swallow men.
My death to him is but a merriment,
And he will murder me to make him sport.

56–86 *Conflicting . . . but dead* This impressive soliloquy which (like Mosby's at the opening of Scene VIII), strikingly reveals the conflicting emotions within the character is not
found in Holinshed's narrative, though Wine (p. xli) suggests that the playwright might
have been inspired by the marginal gloss added to the second edition of the *Chronicles*,
'Note here the force of feare and a troubled conscience', observing that although
'Holinshed in several places points out Michael's fear of Black Will . . . the chronicler
never endows him with even a suggestion of the "troubled conscience" '.

60 *censure* pronounce judgement on

72 *boltered* ed. (bolstred Qq) in tangled knots, or matted with congealed blood (cf. *Macbeth*,
IV.i, 123, 'blood-bolter'd Banquo').

75 *Insulting* Exulting *thee* Q3 (there Q1–2) *peck* heap

80 *detect* reveal, disclose

He comes, he comes! Ah, Master Franklin, help!   85
Call up the neighbours or we are but dead.

Here enters FRANKLIN *and* ARDEN

FRANKLIN

What dismal outcry calls me from my rest?

ARDEN

What hath occasioned such a fearful cry?
Speak, Michael! Hath any injured thee?

MICHAEL

Nothing, sir; but as I fell asleep   90
Upon the threshold, leaning to the stairs,
I had a fearful dream that troubled me,
And in my slumber thought I was beset
With murderer thieves that came to rifle me.
My trembling joints witness my inward fear.   95
I crave your pardons for disturbing you.

ARDEN

So great a cry for nothing I ne'er heard.
What, are the doors fast locked and all things safe?

MICHAEL

I cannot tell; I think I locked the doors.

ARDEN

I like not this, but I'll go see myself.   100

                    [*He tries the doors*]

Ne'er trust me but the doors were all unlocked.
This negligence not half contenteth me.
Get you to bed, and if you love my favour
Let me have no more such pranks as these.
Come, Master Franklin, let us go to bed.   105

FRANKLIN

Ay, by my faith; the air is very cold.
Michael, farewell; I pray thee dream no more.

                    Exeunt

---

91 *leaning to* leaning against
94 *rifle* rob
100 s.d. Presumably Arden moves to the doors at the back of the stage.
106 *by* Q2–3 (be Q1)
107 s.d. So Q2–3. After l. 106 in Q1

SCENE V

Here enters [BLACK] WILL, GREENE, *and* SHAKEBAG

SHAKEBAG

    Black night hath hid the pleasures of the day,
    And sheeting darkness overhangs the earth
    And with the black fold of her cloudy robe
    Obscures us from the eyesight of the world,
    In which sweet silence such as we triumph.   5
    The lazy minutes linger on their time,
    Loth to give due audit to the hour,
    Till in the watch our purpose be complete.
    And Arden sent to everlasting night.
    Greene, get you gone and linger here about,   10
    And at some hour hence come to us again,
    Where we will give you instance of his death.

GREENE

    Speed to my wish whose will so'er says no;
    And so I'll leave you for an hour or two.   *Exit* GREENE

BLACK WILL

    I tell thee, Shakebag, would this thing were done;   15
    I am so heavy that I can scarce go.
    This drowsiness in me bodes little good.

SHAKEBAG

    How now, Will, become a precisian?
    Nay, then, let's go sleep when bugs and fears

1–5 *Black . . . triumph* These lines may perhaps seem strange coming from Shakebag, but
    the playwright's primary concern here is to establish the *mood* of this night scene as
    effectively as possible.
  2 *sheeting* enfolding, covering
  8 *watch* one of the periods into which the night was divided.
 12 *instance* evidence
 13 *speed* success
 18 *precisian* puritan
 19 *bugs* bugbears, imaginary terrors

Shall kill our courages with their fancy's work.   20

BLACK WILL

Why, Shakebag, thou mistakes me much
And wrongs me too in telling me of fear.
Wert not a serious thing we go about,
It should be slipped till I had fought with thee
To let thee know I am no coward, I.   25
I tell thee, Shakebag, thou abusest me.

SHAKEBAG

Why, thy speech bewrayed an inly kind of fear,
And savoured of a weak, relenting spirit.
Go forward now in that we have begun,
And afterwards attempt me when thou darest.   30

BLACK WILL

And if I do not, heaven cut me off!
But let that pass, and show me to this house,
Where thou shalt see I'll do as much as Shakebag.

SHAKEBAG

This is the door [*He tries it*]—but soft, methinks 'tis shut.
The villain Michael hath deceived us.   35

BLACK WILL

Soft, let me see. Shakebag, 'tis shut indeed.
Knock with thy sword; perhaps the slave will hear.

SHAKEBAG

It will not be; the white-livered peasant
Is gone to bed and laughs us both to scorn.

BLACK WILL

And he shall buy his merriment as dear   40
As ever coistrel bought so little sport.

---

20 *fancy's* ed. (fancies Qq)
  fancy's work effect on our imaginations
22 *telling* accusing
24 *slipped* put off
27 *bewrayed* revealed, betrayed
30 *attempt* try your luck with, engage
34 *the door* as in the previous scene (1. 100) one of the doors at the back of the stage, though
  now imagined seen from the outside. The change from interior to exterior scene is
  thereby easily defined
38 *white-livered* cowardly. Cf. 'the liver white and pale, which is the badge of pusillanimity
  and cowardice' (*2 Henry IV*, IV.iii, 103–4).
41 *coistrel* knave (see 1. 59 for variant spelling)

Ne'er let this sword assist me when I need,
But rust and canker after I have sworn,
If I, the next time that I meet the hind,
Lop not away his leg, his arm, or both.   45

SHAKEBAG
And let me never draw a sword again.
Nor prosper in the twilight, cockshut light,
When I would fleece the wealthy passenger,
But lie and languish in a loathsome den,
Hated and spit at by the goers-by,   50
And in that death may die unpitied
If I, the next time that I meet the slave,
Cut not the nose from off the coward's face
And trample on it for this villainy.

BLACK WILL
Come, let's go seek out Greene; I know he'll swear.   55

SHAKEBAG
He were a villain and he would not swear.
'Twould make a peasant swear amongst his boys,
That ne'er durst say before but 'yea' and 'no',
To be thus flouted of a coisterel.

BLACK WILL
Shakebag, let's seek out Greene, and in the morning,   60
At the alehouse 'butting Arden's house,
Watch the out-coming of that prick-eared cur,
And then let me alone to handle him.

Exeunt

---

44 *hind* fellow, servant
47 *cockshut light* 'the close of the evening at which time poultry go to roost' (Johnson).
    Florio's definition (*A Worlde of Wordes,* London, 1598), 'when a man cannot discerne a
    dog from a wolfe' is exactly in keeping with the mood of the speech and scene.
48 *passenger* traveller on foot
57 Sturgess considers the line 'feeble', and is 'tempted to read "pedant" (= schoolteacher) for
    "peasant".' (Qq read *pesant*.)
62 *prick-eared* having pointed ears

SCENE VI

Here enters ARDEN, FRANKLIN, *and* MICHAEL

ARDEN

Sirrah, get you back to Billingsgate
And learn what time the tide will serve our turn.
Come to us in Paul's. First go make the bed,
And afterwards go hearken for the flood.

Exit MICHAEL

Come, Master Franklin, you shall go with me.   5
This night I dreamed that being in a park,
A toil was pitched to overthrow the deer,
And I upon a little rising hill
Stood whistly watching for the herd's approach.
Even there, methoughts, a gentle slumber took me,   10
And summoned all my parts to sweet repose.
But in the pleasure of this golden rest
An ill-thewed foster had removed the toil,
And rounded me with that beguiling home
Which late, methought, was pitched to cast the deer.   15
With that he blew an evil-sounding horn,
And at the noise another herdman came
With falchion drawn, and bent it at my breast,
Crying aloud, 'Thou art the game we seek.'
With this I waked and trembled every joint,   20
Like one obscured in a little bush
That sees a lion foraging about,

---

1 *Billingsgate* 'The principal of the old water-gates of London, on the north side of the Thames, east of London Bridge. . . . It was a usual landing place for travellers from abroad or from the lower reaches of the Thames' (Sugden).
7 *toil* net
9 *whistly* silently
13 *ill-thewed* ill-natured
   foster forester
14 *rounded . . . home* trapped me with the net
15 *cast* overthrow
18 *falchion* (fauchon Qq) a curved broad-sword with the edge on the convex side (cf. *Richard III,* I.ii, 94–5, 'Thy murd'rous falchion smoking in his blood;/The which thou once didst bend against her breast').
   bent aimed

And when the dreadful forest king is gone,
He pries about with timorous suspect
Throughout the thorny casements of the brake,   25
And will not think his person dangerless,
But quakes and shivers though the cause be gone.
So trust me, Franklin, when I did awake
I stood in doubt whether I waked or no,
Such great impression took this fond surprise.   30
God grant this vision bedeem me any good.

FRANKLIN

This fantasy doth rise from Michael's fear,
Who being awaked with the noise he made,
His troubled senses yet could take no rest;
And this, I warrant you, procured your dream.   35

ARDEN

It may be so; God frame it to the best!
But oftentimes my dreams presage too true.

FRANKLIN

To such as note their nightly fantasies,
Some one in twenty may incur belief.
But use it not; 'tis but a mockery.   40

ARDEN

Come, Master Franklin, we'll now walk in Paul's,
And dine together at the ordinary,
And by my man's direction draw to the quay
And with the tide go down to Faversham.
Say, Master Franklin, shall it not be so?   45

FRANKLIN

At your good pleasure, sir; I'll bear you company.

Exeunt

---

24 *suspect* apprehension

25 *brake* thicket. *O.E.D.* (sb. 6I.) notes that the word can also mean 'trap or snare'.

27 *shivers* Q3 (shewers Q1–2)

30 *took . . . surprise* this foolish terror made upon me

31 *bedeem . . . good* fortells no danger for me

32–5 *This fantasy . . . your dream* Cf. Arden himself to Alice in Scene I (1. 74), 'there is no credit in a dream.'

36 *frame* bring to pass

40 *use it not* do not engage in such *a* practice

43 *quay* the wharf at Billingsgate. From there Arden and Franklin would take the barge that plied daily between Billingsgate and Gravesend. The fare was twopence.

SCENE VII

Here enters MICHAEL *at one door.*
Here enters GREENE, [BLACK] WILL, *and* SHAKEBAG *at another door*

BLACK WILL
Draw, Shakebag, for here's that villain Michael.
GREENE
First, Will, let's hear what he can say.
BLACK WILL
Speak, milksop slave, and never after speak!
MICHAEL
For God's sake, sirs, let me excuse myself,
For here I swear by heaven and earth and all,   5
I did perform the outmost of my task,
And left the doors unbolted and unlocked.
But see the chance: Franklin and my master
Were very late conferring in the porch,
And Franklin left his napkin where he sat,   10
With certain gold knit in it, as he said.
Being in bed he did bethink himself,
And coming down he found the doors unshut.
He locked the gates and brought away the keys,
For which offence my master rated me.   15
But now I am going to see what flood it is,
For with the tide my master will away,
Where you may front him well on Rainham Down,

3 *milksop* cowardly
6 *outmost* utmost
8 *chance* mischance
10 *napkin* handkerchief
11 *knit* tied up
15 *rated* berated
18 *front* Q3 (frons Q1–2) confront
    Rainham Down the open countryside around Rainham, a village in Kent, about 5 miles
    from Rochester on the road to Faversham. 'The road from Gravesend to Dover was
    infested by tramps, highwaymen, and ruffians of every sort, and the solitary traveller
    can never have been safe . . . Exposed places like Gad's Hill and Rainham Down were
    notoriously dangerous' (Cust, p. 125).

A place well-fitting such a stratagem.

BLACK WILL

Your excuse hath somewhat mollified my choler.   20

Why now, Greene, 'tis better now nor e'er it was.

GREENE

But, Michael, is this true?

MICHAEL

As true as I report it to be true.

SHAKEBAG

Then, Michael, this shall be your penance:

To feast us all at the Salutation,   25

Where we will plot our purpose thoroughly.

GREENE

And, Michael, you shall bear no news of this tide

Because they two may be in Rainham Down

Before your master.

MICHAEL

Why, I'll agree to anything you'll have me,   30

So you will except of my company.

Exeunt

---

21 *nor* than

25 *Salutation* a tavern in Newgate Street. 'The sign probably represented the meeting between Gabriel and the Virgin Mary' (Sugden).

26 *plot* ed. (plat Qq)

31 *except* Q1–2. (accept Q3). Either reading is possible. Q1–2 reading is supported by Michael's wish (III.178) not to be seen in the cut-throats' company. The attempt on Arden's life in Scene V failed, however, only because Michael did not perform all he had promised, and now he might be more likely to want to ingratiate himself with the murderers. *O.E.D.* cites an example (1635) *of except* used mistakenly for *accept* which might lend further support to Q3's reading.

SCENE VIII

Here enters MOSBY

MOSBY

Disturbed thoughts drives me from company
And dries my marrow with their watchfulness.
Continual trouble of my moody brain
Feebles my body by excess of drink
And nips me as the bitter north-east wind   5
Doth check the tender blossoms in the spring.
Well fares the man, howe'er his cates do taste,
That tables not with foul suspicion;
And he but pines amongst his delicates
Whose troubled mind is stuffed with discontent.   10
My golden time was when I had no gold.
Though then I wanted, yet I slept secure;
My daily toil begat me night's repose,
My night's repose made daylight fresh to me.
But since I climbed the top bough of the tree   15
And sought to build my nest among the clouds,
Each gentlest airy gale doth shake my bed

7 *cates* delicacies, choice food
8 *tables* dines
9 *delicates* usually glossed as 'delicacies' or 'choice food', but *O.E.D.* IV.B.2† a., 'luxuries, delights' is possibly more appropriate, as Mosby develops the sense of his life of material well-being.
12 *Though* Q2–3 (Thought Q1)
17 *Each gentlest airy gale* ed. (Each gentle stary gaile Qq) This emendation (also accepted by Sturgess) was proposed by P. A. McElwaine in '*Arden of Feversham', N. & Q.* 11th ser., II (1910), p. 226, on the grounds that "Each gentlest" is not un-Elizabethan, and whether the *i* in "gaile" is a compositor's misplacement of the *i* in "airy" or not, would not much matter. A loose orthography might spell "airy" as "ary".... "Gale" ... just means a zephyr. "Airy" would emphasize the gentleness of the gale which disturbs one "Whose troubled mind is stuffed with discontent".' Wine emends to *starry* (first proposed by Jacob) but I am not as convinced as he is by R. D. Cornelius's explanation of how a 'gale blowing among the stars' is an appropriate image for Mosby to use (see 'Mosbie's "Stary Gaile" ', *Philological Quarterly*, IX, 1930, p. 72).

And makes me dread my downfall to the earth.
But whither doth contemplation carry me?
The way I seek to find, where pleasure dwells,   20
Is hedged behind me that I cannot back
But needs must on although to danger's gate.
Then, Arden, perish thou by that decree,
For Greene doth ear the land and weed thee up
To make my harvest nothing but pure corn.   25
And for his pains I'll heave him up awhile
And, after, smother him to have his wax;
Such bees as Greene must never live to sting.
Then is there Michael and the painter too,
Chief actors to Arden's overthrow,   30
Who, when they shall see me sit in Arden's seat,
They will insult upon me for my meed,
Or fright me by detecting of his end.
I'll none of that, for I can cast a bone
To make these curs pluck out each other's throat,   35
And then am I sole ruler of mine own.
Yet Mistress Arden lives; but she's myself,
And holy church rites make us two but one.
But what for that I may not trust you, Alice?
You have supplanted Arden for my sake,   40
And will extirpen me to plant another.
'Tis fearful sleeping in a serpent's bed,
And I will cleanly rid my hands of her.

Here enters ALICE [*with a prayerbook*]

24 *ear* plough
26 *heave him up* extol him
27 *smother . . . wax* refers to the practice of smoking out bees in order to obtain the wax and honey from the hive.
32 *meed* reward
34 *a bone* i.e., Susan.
37–8 *Yet Mistress . . . but one* According to Holinshed, Alice and Mosby had promised 'to be in all points as man and wife togither, and therevpon they both receiued the sacrament on a sundaie at London, openlie in a church there.' The playwright makes no specific reference to this event, though Arden refers (I, 17–18) to Mosby wearing the ring 'Which at our marriage day the priest put on', and Mosby twice refers to himself as Alice's 'husband' (I.638 and XIV.275) in Alice's presence.
41 *extirpen* root out, destroy

But here she comes, and I must flatter her.
How now, Alice! What, sad and passionate?   45
Make me partaker of thy pensiveness;
Fire divided burns with lesser force.

ALICE

But I will dam that fire in my breast
Till by the force thereof my part consume.
Ah, Mosby!   50

MOSBY

Such deep pathaires, like to a cannon's burst
Discharged against a ruinated wall,
Breaks my relenting heart in thousand pieces.
Ungentle Alice, thy sorrow is my sore;
Thou know'st it well, and 'tis thy policy   55
To forge distressful looks to wound a breast
Where lies a heart that dies when thou art sad.
It is not love that loves to anger love.

ALICE

It is not love that loves to murder love.

MOSBY

How mean you that?   60

ALICE

Thou knowest how dearly Arden loved me.

MOSBY

And then?

ALICE

And then—conceal the rest, for 'tis too bad.
Lest that my words be carried with the wind
And published in the world to both our shames.   65
I pray thee, Mosby, let our springtime wither;
Our harvest else will yield but loathsome weeds.
Forget, I pray thee, what hath passed betwixt us,
For now I blush and tremble at the thoughts.

---

45 *passionate* sorrowful
48–9 'I will suppress the passion that I have for you until by force of its own violence it
consumes itself and disappears' (Wine). Cf. I.207–8.
51 *pathaires* sad and passionate outbursts. The word does not appear in the *O.E.D.*, but
P. Simpson (*Modern Language Review*, I, 1906, pp. 326–7), has proved its authenticity,
citing another usage in W. Smith's *The Hector of Germanie*, 1615.
52 *ruinated* ruined
57 *when* Q2–3 (where Q1)

MOSBY

What, are you changed? 70

ALICE

Ay, to my former happy life again;
From title of an odious strumpet's name
To honest Arden's wife—not Arden's honest wife.
Ha, Mosby, 'tis thou hast rifled me of that,
And made me sland'rous to all my kin. 75
Even in my forehead is thy name engraven,
A mean artificer, that low-born name.
I was bewitched; woe worth the hapless hour.
And all the causes that enchanted me.

MOSBY

Nay, if thou ban, let me breathe curses forth, 80
And, if you stand so nicely at your fame,
Let me repent the credit I have lost.
I have neglected matters of import
That would have stated me above thy state,
Forslowed advantages, and spurned at time. 85
Ay, Fortune's right hand Mosby hath forsook
To take a wanton giglot by the left.
I left the marriage of an honest maid
Whose dowry would have weighed down all thy wealth,
Whose beauty and demeanour far exceeded thee. 90
This certain good I lost for changing bad,
And wrapped my credit in thy company.
I was bewitched—that is no theme of thine!—
And thou unhallowed hast enchanted me.
But I will break thy spells and exorcisms, 95

---

73 *honest wife* chaste wife. The second part of the line is clearly in response to, or anticipation of, Mosby's reaction to her change of heart.
78 *woe worth* a curse upon
   hapless unfortunate
80 *ban* curse
81 *stand so nicely at* insist so fastidiously on
   fame honour, reputation
84 *stated . . . state* raised me above your rank
85 *Forslowed* Wasted
87 *giglot* lewd, worthless woman
94 *unhallowed* wicked
95 *exorcisms* spells

And put another sight upon these eyes
That showed my heart a raven for a dove.
Thou art not fair, I viewed thee not till now;
Thou art not kind, till now I knew thee not.
And now the rain hath beaten off thy gilt   100
Thy worthless copper shows thee counterfeit.
It grieves me not to see how foul thou art,
But mads me that ever I thought thee fair.
Go, get thee gone, a copesmate for thy hinds!
I am too good to be thy favourite.   105

ALICE

Ay, now I see, and too soon find it true,
Which often hath been told me by my friends,
That Mosby loves me not but for my wealth,
Which too incredulous I ne'er believed.
Nay, hear me speak, Mosby, a word or two;   110
I'll bite my tongue if it speak bitterly.
Look on me, Mosby, or I'll kill myself;
Nothing shall hide me from thy stormy look.
If thou cry war there is no peace for me.
I will do penance for offending thee   115
And burn this prayerbook, where I here use
The holy word that had converted me.
See, Mosby, I will tear away the leaves,
And all the leaves, and in this golden cover
Shall thy sweet phrases and thy letters dwell,   120
And thereon will I chiefly meditate
And hold no other sect but such devotion.
Wilt thou not look? Is all thy love o'erwhelmed?
Wilt thou not hear? What malice stops thine ears?
Why speaks thou not? What silence ties thy tongue? 125
Thou hast been sighted as the eagle is,
And heard as quickly as the fearful hare,
And spoke as smoothly as an orator,

104 *copesmate* companion (in contemptuous sense)
109–10 *Which too . . . or two* Alice's change of direction in the speech is so abrupt that it
    must be prompted by some definite action on Mosby's part: perhaps he goes to leave.
116 *where* wherein
122 *hold . . . sect* keep no other religious faith
127 *quickly* keenly, sharply

When I have bid thee hear, or see, or speak.
And art thou sensible in none of these? 130
Weigh all thy good turns with this little fault
And I deserve not Mosby's muddy looks.
A fount once troubled is not thickened still;
Be clear again, I'll ne'er more trouble thee.

MOSBY

Oh, no, I am a base artificer, 135
My wings are feathered for a lowly flight.
Mosby? Fie, no! Not for a thousand pound.
Make love to you? Why, 'tis unpardonable;
We beggars must not breathe where gentles are.

ALICE

Sweet Mosby is as gentle as a king, 140
And I too blind to judge him otherwise.
Flowers do sometimes spring in fallow lands,
Weeds in gardens, roses grow on thorns;
So whatso'er my Mosby's father was,
Himself is valued gentle by his worth. 145

MOSBY

Ah, how you women can insinuate,
And clear a trespass with your sweet-set tongue.
I will forget this quarrel, gentle Alice,
Provided I'll be tempted so no more.

Here enters BRADSHAW

130 *sensible* capable of feeling, expressing, or perceiving
131 *thy . . . turns* i.e., all the good turns I've done for you.
133 *A fount once troubled* ed. (A fence of trouble Qq) This emendation was proposed by W. Headlam in *The Athanaeum*, 26 December 1903, who argued that 'the text arose from writing or printing "A fonce troubled" instead of "A font on[ce] troubled." M.P. Jackson (p. 50), cites a Shakespearean parallel (*Troilus and Cressida*, III.iii, 310–11): 'My mind is troubled, like a fountain stirred, And I myself not see the bottom of it.' *still* for ever
139 *gentles* of gentle birth or rank
140 *gentle* noble
145 *is* ed. (not in Qq)
147 *clear a trespass* acquit (yourselves)

ALICE

Then with thy lips seal up this new-made match. 150

MOSBY

Soft, Alice, for here comes somebody.

ALICE

How now, Bradshaw, what's the news with you?

BRADSHAW

I have little news, but here's a letter.

That Master Greene importuned me to give you.

ALICE

Go in, Bradshaw; call for a cup of beer. 155

'Tis almost suppertime; thou shalt stay with us.

Exit [BRADSHAW]

Then she reads the letter

'We have missed of our purpose at London, but shall

perform it by the way. We thank our neighbour Bradshaw.

Yours, Richard Greene.'

How likes my love the tenor of this letter? 160

MOSBY

Well, were his date complete and expired.

ALICE

Ah, would it were! Then comes my happy hour.

Till then my bliss is mixed with bitter gall.

Come, let us in to shun suspicion.

MOSBY

Ay, to the gates of death to follow thee. 165

Exeunt

156 s.d. Q2–3; after l. 155 Q1.

157 The letter was written, of course, in Scene II (while Bradshaw was asking Black Will for information), and before the failed attempts on Arden's life in Scenes III and V.

SCENE IX

Here enters GREENE, [BLACK] WILL, *and* SHAKEBAG

SHAKEBAG

    Come, Will, see thy tools be in a readiness.
    Is not thy powder dank, or will thy flint strike fire?

BLACK WILL

    Then ask me if my nose be on my face,
    Or whether my tongue be frozen in my mouth.
    Zounds, here's a coil!   5
    You were best swear me on the intergatories
    How many pistols I have took in hand,
    Or whether I love the smell of gunpowder,
    Or dare abide the noise the dag will make,
    Or will not wink at flashing of the fire.   10
    I pray thee, Shakebag, let this answer thee,
    That I have took more purses in this Down
    Than e'er thou handlest pistols in thy life.

SHAKEBAG

    Ay, haply thou hast picked more in a throng;
    But should I brag what booties I have took,   15
    I think the overplus that's more than thine
    Would mount to a greater sum of money
    Than either thou or all thy kin are worth.
    Zounds, I hate them as I hate a toad
    That carry a muscado in their tongue   20
    And scarce a hurting weapon in their hand.

BLACK WILL

    Oh Greene, intolerable!
    It is not for mine honour to bear this.
    Why, Shakebag, I did serve the king at Boulogne,
    And thou canst brag of nothing that thou has done.   25

---

  5 *coil* fuss
  6 *intergatories* syncopated form of *interrogatories:* questions 'formally put to an accused person or witness' (*O.E.D.*)
  9 *dag* pistol
10 *wink* blink
20 *muscado* ?musket

SHAKEBAG

Why, so can Jack of Faversham,
That sounded for a fillip on the nose,
When he that gave it him holloed in his ear,
And he supposed a cannon-bullet hit him.

Then they fight

GREENE

I pray you, sirs, list to Aesop's talk: 30
Whilst two stout dogs were striving for a bone,
There comes a cur and stole it from them both;
So, while you stand striving on these terms of manhood,
Arden escapes us and deceives us all.

SHAKEBAG

Why, he begun.

BLACK WILL   And thou shalt find I'll end.   35
I do but slip it until better time.
But if I do forget—

Then he kneels down and holds up his hands to heaven

GREENE

Well, take your fittest standings, and once more
Lime your twigs to catch this weary bird.
I'll leave you, and at your dag's discharge   40
Make towards, like the longing water-dog
That coucheth till the fowling-piece be off,
Then seizeth on the prey with eager mood.

---

27 *sounded* swooned, fainted
   fillip sharp blow with the fist
28 *holloed* bellowed
30 *Aesop's talk* References to the fables of Aesop (a Greek slave who is supposed to have lived in the sixth century B.C.)) are common in Elizabethan drama. See also VIII.34–5.
31 *stout* valiant
38 *fittest standings* See III.36n.
39 *weary* wearisome or tedious (because it is taking much longer to kill Arden than Greene had anticipated).
   Lime . . . bird Birdlime was a sticky substance spread (or limed) on branches to catch birds.
42 *coucheth* lies down
   fowling piece A light gun used for shooting wild fowl, which would be retrieved by the *water-dog*.

Ah, might I see him stretching forth his limbs
As I have seen them beat their wings ere now.   45
SHAKEBAG
Why, that thou shalt see if he come this way.
GREENE
Yes, that he doth, Shakebag, I warrant thee.
But brawl not when I am gone in any case,
But, sirs, be sure to speed him when he comes;
And in that hope I'll leave you for an hour.   *Exit* GREENE   50

[BLACK WILL *and* SHAKEBAG *take up their positions*]
Here enters ARDEN, FRANKLIN, *and* MICHAEL

MICHAEL
'Twere best that I went back to Rochester.
The horse halts downright; it were not good
He travelled in such pain to Faversham.
Removing of a shoe may haply help it.
ARDEN
Well, get you back to Rochester; but, sirrah, see ye   55
Overtake us ere we come to Rainham Down,
For it will be very late ere we get home.
MICHAEL
[*Aside*] Ay, God he knows, and so doth Will and Shakebag,
That thou shalt never go further than that Down;
And therefore have I pricked the horse on purpose,   60
Because I would not view the massacre.   *Exit* MICHAEL
ARDEN
Come, Master Franklin, onwards with your tale.

---

45 *them* i.e., the waterfowl
50 s.d. possibly behind one of the stage pillars
52 *halts downright* limps badly
56 Black Will and Shakebag, who are also on stage, are, of course, already at Rainham Down.
Arden and Franklin make their way there by walking round the stage while Franklin tells
his tale and Black Will and Shakebag remain concealed. The murderers emerge as Arden
and Franklin approach ('Stand close, Will, I hear them coming') but are thwarted by the
sudden appearance through the rear doors of Lord Cheiny and his retinue, and by Lord
Cheiny evidently placing himself (unintentionally) between the murderers and Arden.
60 *pricked the horse* i.e., pierced the horse's foot to the quick, thereby laming it

FRANKLIN

    I assure you, sir, you task me much.

    A heavy blood is gathered at my heart,

    And on the sudden is my wind so short   65

    As hindereth the passage of my speech.

    So fierce a qualm yet ne'er assailed me.

ARDEN

    Come, Master Franklin, let us go on softly.

    The annoyance of the dust or else some meat

    You ate at dinner cannot brook with you.   70

    I have been often so and soon amended.

FRANKLIN

    Do you remember where my tale did leave?

ARDEN

    Ay, where the gentleman did check his wife.

FRANKLIN

    She being reprehended for the fact,

    Witness produced that took her with the deed,   75

    Her glove brought in which there she left behind,

    And many other assured arguments,

    Her husband asked her whether it were not so.

ARDEN

    Her answer then? I wonder how she looked,

    Having forsworn it with such vehement oaths,   80

    And at the instant so approved upon her.

FRANKLIN

    First did she cast her eyes down to the earth,

    Watching the drops that fell amain from thence;

    Then softly draws she forth her handkerchief,

    And modestly she wipes her tear-stained face;   85

    Then hemmed she out, to clear her voice should seem,

    And with a majesty addressed herself

---

64 *heavy* oppressive

67 *fierce* Q3 (ferse Q1–2)

68 *softly* gently, slowly

70 *brook with you* Q2–3 (brooke you Q1) agree with you

72 *leave* leave off

73 *check* reprimand, reprove

75 *took . . . deed* caught her in the act

77 *arguments* evidence

81 *approved upon* proved against

To encounter all their accusations.—
Pardon me, Master Arden, I can no more;
This fighting at my heart makes short my wind.   90
ARDEN
Come, we are almost now at Rainham Down.
Your pretty tale beguiles the weary way;
I would you were in state to tell it out.
SHAKEBAG
[*Aside*] Stand close, Will, I hear them coming.

Here enters LORD CHEINY *with his* MEN

BLACK WILL
[*Aside*] Stand to it, Shakebag, and be resolute.   95
LORD CHEINY
Is it so near night as it seems,
Or will this black-faced evening have a shower?
                                        [*Seeing* ARDEN]
What, Master Arden? You are well met.
I have longed this fortnight's day to speak with you.
You are a stranger, man, in the Isle of Sheppey.   100
ARDEN
Your honour's always! Bound to do you service.
LORD CHEINY
Come you from London and ne'er a man with you?
ARDEN
My man's coming after,
But here's my honest friend that came along with me.
LORD CHEINY
[*To* FRANKLIN] My Lord Protector's man I take you to be.   105
FRANKLIN
Ay, my good lord, and highly bound to you.
LORD CHEINY
You and your friend come home and sup with me.
ARDEN
I beseech your honour pardon me;
I have made a promise to a gentleman,
My honest friend, to meet him at my house.
The occasion is great, or else would I wait on you.   110

88 *encounter* counter, dispute

LORD CHEINY

    Will you come tomorrow and dine with me?
    And bring your honest friend along with you.
    I have divers matters to talk with you about.

ARDEN

    Tomorrow we'll wait upon your honour.   115

LORD CHEINY

    One of you stay my horse at the top of the hill.

                                [Seeing BLACK WILL]

    What, Black Will! For whose purse wait you?
    Thou wilt be hanged in Kent when all is done.

BLACK WILL

    Not hanged, God save your honour.
    I am your beadsman, bound to pray for you.   120

LORD CHEINY

    I think thou ne'er saidest prayer in all thy life
    One of you give him a crown.
    And, sirrah, leave this kind of life;
    If thou beest 'tainted for a penny matter
    And come in question, surely thou wilt truss.   125
    Come, Master Arden, let us be going;
    Your way and mine lies four mile together.

                                  Exeunt

                Manet BLACK WILL *and* SHAKEBAG

BLACK WILL

    The Devil break all your necks at four miles' end!
    Zounds, I could kill myself for very anger!
    His lordship chops me in even when   130
    My dag was levelled at his heart.
    I would his crown were molten down his throat.

SHAKEBAG

    Arden, thou hast wondrous holy luck.
    Did ever man escape as thou hast done?

---

120 *beadsman* one paid to pray for the others. Also used as a term to address superiors, cf.
     'your humble servant'.
124–5 'If you are accused of even the most trivial offence and are brought to trial, you'll
     hang for certain.' *truss* hang
130 *chops me in* suddenly intervenes
131 *his* i.e., Arden's
132 *his . . . his* i.e., Cheiny's

Well, I'll discharge my pistol at the sky,   135
For by this bullet Arden might not die.

Here enters GREENE

GREENE

What, is he down? Is he dispatched?

SHAKEBAG

Ay, in health towards Faversham to shame us all.

GREENE

The devil he is! Why, sirs, how escaped he?

SHAKEBAG

When we were ready to shoot   140
Comes my Lord Cheiny to prevent his death.

GREENE

The Lord of Heaven hath preserved him.

BLACK WILL

The Lord of Heaven a fig! The Lord Cheiny hath
    preserved him,
And bids him to a feast, to his house at Shorlow.
But by the way once more I'll meet with him,   145
And if all the Cheinies in the world say no,
I'll have a bullet in his breast tomorrow.
Therefore come, Greene, and let us to Faversham.

GREENE

Ay, and excuse ourselves to Mistress Arden.
Oh, how she'll chafe when she hears of this!   150

SHAKEBAG

Why, I'll warrant you she'll think we dare not do it.

BLACK WILL

Why then let us go and tell her all the matter,
And plot the news to cut him off tomorrow.

Exeunt

143 *The Lord of Heaven a fig!* ed. (Preserued, a figge, Qq)
    'Will's denial that Arden has been preserved ("Preserued, a figge") is contradictory. He
    should speak some such line as:
        The Lord of Heaven a fig! Lord Cheiny hath
    the quibble being upon the two different kinds of "Lord" ' (Jackson, p. 28).
144 *Shorlow* i.e., Shurland, Lord Cheiny's house on the Isle of Sheppey.
153 *plot* Q3 (plat Q1–2)
    plot the news devise a new plan

SCENE X

Here enters ARDEN *and his wife* [ALICE],
FRANKLIN *and* MICHAEL

ARDEN
    See how the Hours, the guardant of heaven's gate,
    Have by their toil removed the darksome clouds,
    That Sol may well discern the trampled pace
    Wherein he wont to guide his golden car.
    The season fits; come, Franklin, let's away.   5

ALICE
    I thought you did pretend some special hunt
    That made you thus cut short the time of rest.

ARDEN
    It was no chase that made me rise so early,
    But, as I told thee yesternight, to go
    To the Isle of Sheppey, there to dine with my Lord Cheiny,   10
    For so his honour late commanded me.

ALICE
    Ay, such kind husbands seldom want excuses.
    Home is a wild cat to a wand'ring wit.
    The time hath been — would God it were not past —
    That honour's title nor a lord's command   15
    Could once have drawn you from these arms of mine.
    But my deserts or your desires decay,
    Or both; yet if true love may seem desert,
    I merit still to have thy company.

---

1 *the Hours* the daughters of Zeus and Themis, who were the custodians of the gates of Olympus, and who also governed changes in the weather.
  guardant keeper
3 *Sol* the sun, personified
  discern Q2–3 (deserne; discerne); (deserue Q1)
  pace path
6 *pretend* intend (though considering Alice's feelings towards Arden, the sub-text of the word may well be 'to use as a pretext').
11 *late* recently
12 *want* lack
17 *deserts* merits, good qualities
  desires ed. (deserues Q1; desernes Q2; deserves Q3)'
18 *desert* deserving

FRANKLIN

    Why, I pray you, sir, let her go along with us;   20

    I am sure his honour will welcome her,

    And us the more for bringing her along.

ARDEN

    Content. [*To* MICHAEL] Sirrah, saddle your mistress' nag.

ALICE

    No. Begged favour merits little thanks.

    If I should go our house would run away   25

    Or else be stol'n; therefore I'll stay behind.

ARDEN

    Nay, see how mistaking you are. I pray thee, go.

ALICE

    No, no, not now.

ARDEN

    Then let me leave thee satisfied in this:

    That time nor place nor persons alter me,

    But that I hold thee dearer than my life.   30

ALICE

    That will be seen by your quick return,

ARDEN

    And that shall be ere night and if I live.

    Farewell, sweet Alice; we mind to sup with thee.

                                      Exit ALICE

FRANKLIN

    Come, Michael, are our horses ready?   35

MICHAEL

    Ay, your horses are ready, but I am not ready, for I have lost
my purse with six-and-thirty shillings in it, with taking up of
my master's nag.

FRANKLIN

    Why, I pray you, let us go before,

    Whilst he stays behind to seek his purse.   40

ARDEN

    Go to, sirrah! See you follow us to the Isle of Sheppey,

    To my Lord Cheiny's, where we mean to dine.

                         Exeunt ARDEN *and* FRANKLIN

                                 Manet MICHAEL

33 *and if* if

37 *taking up* 'to bring (a horse, ox, etc.) from pasture into the stable or stall' (*O.E.D.*)

38 *master's* ed. (M. Ql-2; mistres Q3—see l. 23 above)

MICHAEL

So, fair weather after you, for before you lies Black Will and
Shakebag in the broom close, too close for you. They'll be your
ferrymen to long home.   45

Here enters the Painter [CLARKE]

But who is this? The painter, my co-rival, that would needs win
Mistress Susan.

CLARKE

How now, Michael? How doth my mistress and all at home?

MICHAEL

Who? Susan Mosby? She is your mistress, too?

CLARKE

Ay. How doth she and all the rest?   50

MICHAEL

All's well but Susan; she is sick.

CLARKE

Sick? Of what disease?

MICHAEL

Of a great fear.

CLARKE

A fear of what?

MICHAEL

A great fever.   55

CLARKE

A fever! God forbid!

MICHAEL

Yes, faith, and of a lurdan, too, as big as yourself.

CLARKE

Oh, Michael, the spleen prickles you. Go to; you carry an eye
over Mistress Susan.

44 *broom close* enclosed field of shrubs
45 *ferrymen* i.e., Charon, who conveyed the dead souls across the River Styx to Hades.
   to long home i.e., the grave. Cf. the proverb, 'He is gone to his long (last) home' (Tilley,
   H533). 'There is a quibble on "holme", meaning a little island in the river. Arden is about
   to take the ferry to the Isle of Sheppey; Michael says that the two murderers will act as
   his Charon-like ferrymen to a home/holme of a different kind' (Jackson, p. 175).
57 *lurdan* an insult meaning a rogue or loafer, and with a play on the term *feverlurden*, the
   disease of laziness.
58 *spleen* an organ often associated with laughter, but also with heat, ill-temper, and irasci-
   bility, as it was believed to be the seat of melancholy and sudden passions.
   prickles goads
58–9 *carry an eye over* have your eye on, fancy

MICHAEL

Ay, faith, to keep her from the painter. 60

CLARKE

Why more from a painter than from a serving-creature like
yourself?

MICHAEL

Because you painters make but a painting-table of a pretty
wench and spoil her beauty with blotting.

CLARKE

What mean you by that? 65

MICHAEL

Why, that you painters paint lambs in the lining of wenches'
petticoats, and we servingmen put horns to them to make them
become sheep.

CLARKE

Such another word will cost you a cuff or a knock.

MICHAEL

What, with a dagger made of a pencil? Faith, 'tis too weak, and 70
therefore thou too weak to win Susan.

CLARKE

Would Susan's love lay upon this stroke!

Then he breaks MICHAEL's *head*
Here enters MOSBY, GREENE *and* ALICE

ALICE

I'll lay my life this is for Susan's love.
[*To* MICHAEL] Stayed you behind your master to this end?
Have you no other time to brabble in 75

---

63 *painting-table* 'a board or other flat surface on which a picture is painted; hence, the
picture itself (O.E.D., *Table*, sb., †3).

64 *blotting* painting badly; but also with the sense of 'to cast a blot upon a reputation'
(O.E.D.).

66–8 The meaning is obscure. Wine suggests it is a 'proverbial allusion to the horns of the
cuckold', but the idea of sexual rivalry between Clarke and Michael (which parallels that
of Arden and Mosby), is clearer if *horn* is glossed as 'erect penis' (see E. Partridge,
Shakespeare's Bawdy, 1961, p. 129). Michael's taunt, therefore, is that while Clarke is
occupied with decorating Susan's petticoat (the front panel of which would possibly have
been visible), Michael is proving his manhood in a rather more direct manner.

69 *cuff* blow

72 s.d. indicates a stage fight

73 *lay* bet

75 *brabble* brawl

But now, when serious matters are in hand?

[*Exit* MICHAEL]

Say, Clarke, hast thou done the thing thou promised?

CLARKE

Ay, here it is; the very touch is death. [*Exit* CLARKE]

ALICE

Then this, I hope, if all the rest do fail,
Will catch Master Arden   80
And make him wise in death that lived a fool.
Why should he thrust his sickle in our corn,
Or what hath he to do with thee, my love,
Or govern me that am to rule myself?
Forsooth, for credit sake I must leave thee!   85
Nay, he must leave to live that we may love,
May live, may love; for what is life but love?
And love shall last as long as life remains,
And life shall end before my love depart.

MOSBY

Why, what's love without true constancy?   90
Like to a pillar built of many stones,
Yet neither with good mortar well compact,
Nor cement to fasten it in the joints,
But what it shakes with every blast of wind,
And being touched, straight falls unto the earth   95
And buries all his haughty pride in dust.
No, let our love be rocks of adamant
Which time nor place nor tempest can asunder.

GREENE

Mosby, leave protestations now,
And let us bethink us what we have to do.   100
Black Will and Shakebag I have placed
In the broom close, watching Arden's coming.
Let's to them and see what they have done.

Exeunt

76, 78 s.d.s I have suggested these exits as the closing moments of the scene are better
    focused if only Alice, Mosby and Greene remain on stage.
78 *it* i.e. the poisoned crucifix (see I.609ff.)
86 *leave* cease
93 *cement* Q3 (semell Q1–2)

SCENE XI

Here enters ARDEN *and* FRANKLIN

ARDEN

Oh ferryman, where art thou?

Here enters the FERRYMAN

FERRYMAN

Here, here! Go before to the boat, and I will follow you.

ARDEN

We have great haste; I pray thee come away.

FERRYMAN

Fie, what a mist is here!

ARDEN

This mist, my friend, is mystical,   5
Like to a good companion's smoky brain
That was half-drowned with new ale overnight.

FERRYMAN

'Twere pity but his skull were opened to make more chimney
room.

FRANKLIN

Friend, what's thy opinion of this mist?   10

FERRYMAN

I think 'tis like to a curst wife in a little house, that never leaves
her husband till she have driven him out at doors with a wet
pair of eyes. Then looks he as if his house were afire, or some of
his friends dead.

ARDEN

Speaks thou this of thine own experience?   15

FERRYMAN

Perhaps ay, perhaps no; for my wife is as other women are, that
is to say, governed by the moon.

---

8 *but* unless
11 *curst* shrewish
12 *at* of
17 *governed by the moon* cf. proverb, 'As changeful (inconstant) as the moon' (Tilley,
   M1111). Jackson (p. 77) notes the possible allusion to the menstrual cycle (see ll. 24–5
   below).

FRANKLIN

By the moon? How, I pray thee?

FERRYMAN

Nay, thereby lies a bargain, and you shall not have it fresh and   20
fasting.

ARDEN

Yes, I pray thee, good ferryman.

FERRYMAN

Then for this once let it be midsummer moon; but yet my wife
has another moon.

FRANKLIN

Another moon?

FERRYMAN

Ay, and it hath influences and eclipses.   25

ARDEN

Why then, by this reckoning you sometimes play the man in the
moon.

FERRYMAN

Ay, but you had not best to meddle with that moon lest I scratch
you by the face with my bramble-bush.

ARDEN

I am almost stifled with this fog; come, let's away.   30

FRANKLIN

And sirrah, as we go, let us have some more of your bold
yeomanry.

FERRYMAN

Nay, by my troth, sir, but flat knavery.

Exeunt

19–20 *fresh and fasting* for nothing (so Baskervill, cited by Wine)
22 *midsummer moon* 'The lunar month in which Midsummer Day comes; sometimes alluded to as a time when lunacy is supposed to be prevalent' (*O.E.D.*). The
Ferryman seems to be saying: 'Then just this once I'll be mad and tell you the jest for
nothing.'
23 *another moon* i.e., her sexual organs.
25 *influences and eclipses* obvious sexual connotations.
26–7 *man in the moon* again, the sexual allusion is obvious.
29 *bramble bush* Cf. *A Midsummer Night's Dream*, V.i, 250–2, 'All that I have to say, is, to
tell you that the lanthorn is the moon; I, the man i' the moon; this thorn-bush, my
thorn-bush; and this dog, my dog.'
31–2 *bold yeomanry* honest, homely speech

SCENE XII

Here enters [BLACK] WILL *at one door and*
SHAKEBAG *at another*

SHAKEBAG

Oh Will, where art thou?

BLACK WILL

Here, Shakebag, almost in hell's mouth, where I cannot see my
way for smoke.

SHAKEBAG

I pray thee speak still that we may meet by the sound, for I shall
fall into some ditch or other unless my feet see better than my   5
eyes.

BLACK WILL

Didst thou ever see better weather to run away with another
man's wife or play with a wench at potfinger?

SHAKEBAG

No; this were a fine world for chandlers if this weather would
last, for then a man should never dine nor sup without candle-   10
light. But, sirrah Will, what horses are those that passed?

BLACK WILL

Why, didst thou hear any?

SHAKEBAG

Ay, that I did.

BLACK WILL

My life for thine, 'twas Arden and his companion, and then all
our labour's lost.   15

SHAKEBAG

Nay, say not so; for if it be they, they may haply lose their way as
we have done, and then we may chance meet with them.

---

8 *potfinger* obvious sexual allusion (*O.E.D.* quotes Withals *Dictionary*, 1666: 'A potte made
in the mouthe, with one finger, as children vse to do'.)

BLACK WILL

    Come, let us go on like a couple of blind pilgrims.

                  Then SHAKEBAG *falls into a ditch*

SHAKEBAG

    Help, Will, help! I am almost drowned.

Here enters the FERRYMAN

FERRYMAN

    Who's that that calls for help? 20

BLACK WILL

    'Twas none here; 'twas thou thyself.

FERRYMAN

    I came to help him that called for help. Why, how now? Who
    is this that's in the ditch? You are well enough served to go
    without a guide such weather as this!

BLACK WILL

    Sirrah, what companies hath passed your ferry this morning? 25

FERRYMAN

    None but a couple of gentlemen that went to dine at my Lord
    Cheiny's.

BLACK WILL

    Shakebag, did I not tell thee as much?

FERRYMAN

    Why, sir, will you have any letters carried to them?

BLACK WILL

    No, sir; get you gone. 30

FERRYMAN

    Did you ever see such a mist as this?

BLACK WILL

    No, nor such a fool as will rather be hocked than get his way.

---

18 s.d. *a ditch* possibly Shakebag falls through the trap door of the stage (though see G.
    Wickham, *Shakespeare's Dramatic Heritage*, 1969, p. 126). More simply, Shakebag might
    just fall to the floor.
23 *to go* for going
25 *companies* groups of people (Q2 and Q3 read *companions*)
32 *hocked* ed. (hought Qq)

FERRYMAN

    Why, sir, this is no Hock Monday; you are deceived. What's his
    name, I pray you, sir?

SHAKEBAG

    His name is Black Will.   35

FERRYMAN

    I hope to see him one day hanged upon a hill.

Exit FERRYMAN

SHAKEBAG

    See how the sun hath cleared the foggy mist,
    Now we have missed the mark of our intent.

Here enters GREENE, MOSBY, and ALICE

MOSBY

    Black Will and Shakebag, what make you here?
    What, is the deed done? Is Arden dead?   40

BLACK WILL

    What could a blinded man perform in arms?
    Saw you not how till now the sky was dark,
    That neither horse nor man could be discerned?
    Yet did we hear their horses as they passed.

GREENE

    Have they escaped you then and passed the ferry?   45

SHAKEBAG

    Ay, for a while; but here we two will stay,
    And at their coming back meet with them once more.
    Zounds, I was ne'er so toiled in all my life
    In following so slight a task as this.

MOSBY

    How cam'st thou so bewrayed?   50

---

33 *Hock Monday* a festival held the second Monday (and Tuesday) after Easter, during which
   the women caught (or 'hocked') the men, and made them pay a ransom for their
   freedom. (See Bluestone's discussion of the connection of this with the *net* images
   throughout the play, pp. 178–9.)
48 *toiled* exhausted, worn out
50 *berayed* covered in mud

BLACK WILL

With making false footing in the dark;
He needs would follow them without a guide.

ALICE

Here's to pay for a fire and good cheer.
Get you to Faversham, to the Flower-de-Luce,
And rest yourselves until some other time.   55

GREENE

Let me alone; it most concerns my state.

BLACK WILL

Ay, Mistress Arden, this will serve the turn
In case we fall into a second fog.

Exeunt GREENE, [BLACK] WILL *and* SHAKEBAG

MOSBY

These knaves will never do it; let us give it over.

ALICE

First tell me how you like my new device: 60
Soon, when my husband is returning back,
You and I both marching arm in arm,
Like loving friends, we'll meet him on the way,
And boldy beard and brave him to his teeth.
When words grow hot and blows begin to rise,   65
I'll call those cutters forth your tenement,
Who, in a manner to take up the fray,
Shall wound my husband Hornsby to the death.

MOSBY

Ah, fine device! Why, this deserves a kiss.

Exeunt

---

56 *Let me alone* either; 'Leave me alone to deal with them', or: 'Let me be the one to take care of things'.
60 *device* scheme, plan
64 *beard* affront
66 *tenement* dwelling-place
68 *Hornsby* i.e. the cuckold (see XIII.82)

SCENE XIII

Here enters DICK REEDE *and a* SAILOR

SAILOR

    Faith, Dick Reede, it is to little end.
    His conscience is too liberal and he too niggardly.
    To part from anything may do thee good.

REEDE

    He is coming from Shorlow as I understand.
    Here I'll intercept him, for at his house   5
    He never will vouchsafe to speak with me.
    If prayers and fair entreaties will not serve
    Or make no batt'ry in his flinty breast,

Here enters FRANKLIN, ARDEN, *and* MICHAEL

    I'll curse the carl and see what that will do.
    See where he comes to further my intent. —   10
    Master Arden, I am now bound to the sea.
    My coming to you was about the plot of ground
    Which wrongfully you detain from me.
    Although the rent of it be very small,
    Yet will it help my wife and children,   15
    Which here I leave in Faversham, God knows,
    Needy and bare. For Christ's sake, let them have it!

ARDEN

    Franklin, hearest thou this fellow speak?
    That which he craves I dearly bought of him
    Although the rent of it was ever mine.   20
    Sirrah, you that ask these questions,
    If with thy clamorous impeaching tongue
    Thou rail on me as I have heard thou dost,

---

2 *liberal* 'Free from restraint. . . . In 16–17th c. often in a bad sense: unrestrained by pru-
    dence or decorum, licentious' (*O.E.D.*),
9 *carl* miserly fellow

I'll lay thee up so close a twelve month's day
As thou shalt neither see the sun nor moon.   25
Look to it; for, as surely as I live,
I'll banish pity if thou use me thus.

REEDE

What, wilt thou do me wrong and threat me too?
Nay then, I'll tempt thee, Arden; do thy worst.
God, I beseech thee, show some miracle   30
On thee or thine in plaguing thee for this.
That plot of ground which thou detains from me
I speak it in an agony of spirit —
Be ruinous and fatal unto thee!
Either there be butchered by thy dearest friends,   35
Or else be brought for men to wonder at,
Or thou or thine miscarry in that place,
Or there run mad and end thy cursed days.

FRANKLIN

Fie, bitter knave, bridle thine envious tongue;
For curses are like arrows shot upright,   40
Which, falling down, light on the shooter's head.

REEDE

Light where they will! Were I upon the sea,
As oft I have in many a bitter storm,
And saw a dreadful southern flaw at hand,
The pilot quaking at the doubtful storm,   45
And all the sailors praying on their knees,
Even in that fearful time would I fall down
And ask of God, whate'er betide of me,
Vengeance on Arden, or some misevent,
To show the world what wrong the carl hath done.   50
This charge I'll leave with my distressful wife;

---

24 *lay . . . close* imprison you
29 *tempt* provoke
37 *miscarry* come to harm, die
39 *envious* malicious
40–1 Cf. proverb, 'Curses return upon the heads of those that curse' (Tilley, C924).
41 *shooter's* Q3 (sutors Q1–2)
44 *flaw* squall
45 *doubtful* dreaded
49 *misevent* mischance

My children shall be taught such prayers as these.
And thus I go, but leave my curse with thee.

Exeunt REEDE *and* SAILOR

ARDEN

It is the railingest knave in Christendom,
And oftentimes the villain will be mad.   55
It greatly matters not what he says,
But I assure you I ne'er did him wrong.

FRANKLIN

I think so, Master Arden.

ARDEN

Now that our horses are gone home before,
My wife may haply meet me on the way;   60
For God knows she is grown passing kind of late
And greatly changed from the old humour
Of her wonted frowardness,
And seeks by fair means to redeem old faults.

FRANKLIN

Happy the change that alters for the best.   65
But see in any case you make no speech
Of the cheer we had at my Lord Cheiny's —
Although most bounteous and liberal —
For that will make her think herself more wronged
In that we did not carry her along;   70
For sure she grieved that she was left behind.

ARDEN

Come, Franklin, let us strain to mend our pace
And take her unawares, playing the cook,

Here enters ALICE *and* MOSBY [*arm in arm*]

For I believe she'll strive to mend our cheer.

FRANKLIN

Why, there's no better creatures in the world   75
Than women are when they are in good humours.

---

62 *humour* temper, disposition
63 *frowardness* ill-humour
67 *cheer* hospitality
72 *mend* increase

ARDEN

    Who is that? Mosby? What, so familiar?

    Injurious strumpet and thou ribald knave,

    Untwine those arms.

ALICE

    Ay, with a sugared kiss let them untwine.   80

ARDEN

    Ah, Mosby! Perjured beast! Bear this and all!

MOSBY

    And yet no horned beast; the horns are thine.

FRANKLIN

    Oh monstrous! Nay then, 'tis time to draw!

ALICE

    Help! Help! They murder my husband!

Here enters [BLACK] WILL *and* SHAKEBAG

SHAKEBAG

    Zounds, who injures Master Mosby?   85

            [*They fight.* SHAKEBAG *and* MOSBY *are wounded*]

    Help, Will, I am hurt.

MOSBY

    I may thank you, Mistress Arden, for this wound.

           Exeunt MOSBY, [BLACK] WILL, *and* SHAKEBAG

ALICE

    Ah, Arden, what folly blinded thee?

    Ah, jealous harebrain man what hast thou done?

    When we, to welcome thee, intended sport,   90

    Came lovingly to meet thee on thy way,

    Thou drew'st thy sword, enraged with jealousy,

    And hurt thy friend whose thoughts were free from harm;

    All for a worthless kiss and joining arms,

    Both done but merrily to try thy patience.   95

    And me unhappy that devised the jest,

    Which, though begun in sport, yet ends in blood!

FRANKLIN

    Marry, God defend me from such a jest!

78 *ribald* scurrilous

82 *horned beast* i.e., cuckold

ALICE

    Couldst thou not see us friendly smile on thee
    When we joined arms and when I kissed his cheek?   100
    Hast thou not lately found me over-kind?
    Didst thou not hear me cry they murder thee?
    Called I not help to set my husband free?
    No, ears and all were 'witched. Ah me accursed,
    To link in liking with a frantic man!   105
    Henceforth I'll be thy slave, no more thy wife;
    For with that name I never shall content thee.
    If I be merry, thou straightways thinks me light;
    If sad, thou sayest the sullens trouble me;
    If well attired, thou thinks I will be gadding;   110
    If homely, I seem sluttish in thine eye.
    Thus am I still, and shall be while I die,
    Poor wench abused by thy misgovernment.

ARDEN

    But is it for truth that neither thou nor he
    Intendedst malice in your misdemeanour?   115

ALICE

    The heavens can witness of our harmless thoughts.

ARDEN

    Then pardon me, sweet Alice, and forgive this fault;
    Forget but this, and never see the like.
    Impose me penance, and I will perform it;
    For in thy discontent I find a death,   120
    A death tormenting more than death itself.

ALICE

    Nay, hadst thou loved me as thou dost pretend,
    Thou wouldst have marked the speeches of thy friend,
    Who going wounded from the place, he said
    His skin was pierced only through my device.   125
    And if sad sorrow taint thee for this fault
    Thou wouldst have followed him and seen him dressed,
    And cried him mercy whom thou hast misdone;
    Ne'er shall my heart be eased till this be done.

109 *sullens* sulks
112 *still* always
     while until
127 *him* i.e., his wounds
128 *misdone* wronged, injured

ARDEN

    Content thee, sweet Alice, thou shalt have thy will,   130
    Whate'er it be. For that I injured thee
    And wronged my friend, shame scourgeth my offence.
    Come thou thyself and go along with me,
    And be a mediator 'twixt us two.

FRANKLIN

    Why, Master Arden, know you what you do?   135
    Will you follow him that hath dishonoured you?

ALICE

    Why, canst thou prove I have been disloyal?

FRANKLIN

    Why, Mosby taunts your husband with the horn.

ALICE

    Ay, after he had reviled him
    By the injurious name of perjured beast.   140
    He knew no wrong could spite a jealous man
    More than the hateful naming of the horn.

FRANKLIN

    Suppose 'tis true, yet is it dangerous
    To follow him whom he hath lately hurt.

ALICE

    A fault confessed is more than half amends,   145
    But men of such ill spirit as yourself
    Work crosses and debates 'twixt man and wife.

ARDEN

    I pray thee, gentle Franklin, hold thy peace;
    I know my wife counsels me for the best.
    I'll seek out Mosby where his wound is dressed   150
    And salve his hapless quarrel if I may.

                          Exeunt ARDEN *and* ALICE

FRANKLIN

    He whom the devil drives must go perforce.
    Poor gentleman, how soon he is bewitched.
    And yet, because his wife is the instrument,
    His friends must not be lavish in their speech.   155

                                Exit FRANKLIN

---

131 *For that* Because
138 *taunts your* Q3 (traunt you Q1; taunt you Q2)
151 *hapless* unfortunate

SCENE XIV

Here enters [BLACK] WILL, SHAKEBAG, *and* GREENE

BLACK WILL

Sirrah Greene, when was I so long in killing a man?

GREENE

I think we shall never do it; let us give it over.

SHAKEBAG

Nay! Zounds, we'll kill him though we be hanged at his door for
our labour.

BLACK WILL

Thou knowest, Greene, that I have lived in London this twelve   5
years, where I have made some go upon wooden legs for taking
the wall on me; divers with silver noses for saying, 'There goes
Black Will.' I have cracked as many blades as thou hast done
nuts.

GREENE

Oh, monstrous lie!   10

BLACK WILL

Faith, in a manner I have. The bawdy-houses have paid me
tribute; there durst not a whore set up unless she have agreed
with me first for opening her shop windows. For a cross word of
a tapster I have pierced one barrel after another with my dagger
and held him by the ears till all his beer hath run out. In   15
Thames Street a brewer's cart was like to have run over me; I
made no more ado but went to the clerk and cut all the notches
off his tallies and beat them about his head. I and my company
have taken the constable from his watch and carried him about
the fields on a coltstaff. I have broken a sergeant's head with his   20

6–7 *taking the wall* i.e., taking the side of the street nearest the wall (thereby forcing Black
Will into the middle of the street where it was filthiest).

7 *silver noses* i.e. false noses

18 *tallies* ed. (tales Qq)
tallies sticks of wood marked on one side with notches representing the amount of a debt
or payment.

20 *coltstaff* (or cowlstaff): a pole used for carrying a cowl (tub); *O.E.D.* notes, 'It was a
familiar household requisite, and a ready weapon.'
sergeant officer responsible for arresting offenders or summoning them to court.

own mace, and bailed whom I list with my sword and buckler.
All the tenpenny alehouses would stand every morning with a
quart pot in their hand, saying, 'Will it please your worship
drink?' He that had not done so had been sure to have had his
sign pulled down and his lattice borne away the next night. To   25
conclude, what have I not done? Yet cannot do this; doubtless
he is preserved by miracle.

Here enters ALICE *and* MICHAEL

GREENE
Hence, Will; here comes Mistress Arden.
ALICE
Ah, gentle Michael, art thou sure they're friends?
MICHAEL
Why, I saw them when they both shook hands;   30
When Mosby bled he even wept for sorrow,
And railed on Franklin that was cause of all.
No sooner came the surgeon in at doors,
But my master took his purse and gave him money,
And, to conclude, sent me to bring you word   35
That Mosby, Franklin, Bradshaw, Adam Fowle,
With divers of his neighbours and his friends,
Will come and sup with you at our house this night.
ALICE
Ah, gentle Michael, run thou back again,
And when my husband walks into the fair,   40
Bid Mosby steal from him and come to me;
And this night shall thou and Susan be made sure.
MICHAEL
I'll go tell him.
ALICE
And as thou goest, tell John cook of our guests,

---

21 *mace* staff of office
    list wished, chose
22 *tenpenny alehouses* i.e., the keepers of alehouses where ale was sold for tenpence a quart.
23 *their* Q2–3 (his Q1)
25 *lattice* a window of lattice work painted either red or green was the sign of an alehouse.
40 *the fair* i.e., of St Valentine.
44 *John cook* i.e., John, the cook.

And bid him lay it on; spare for no cost.   45

Exit MICHAEL

BLACK WILL

Nay, and there be such cheer, we will bid ourselves. Mistress
Arden, Dick Greene and I do mean to sup with you.

ALICE

And welcome shall you be. Ah, gentlemen,
How missed you of your purpose yesternight?

GREENE

'Twas long of Shakebag, that unlucky villain,   50

SHAKEBAG

Thou dost me wrong; I did as much as any.

BLACK WILL

Nay then, Mistress Alice, I'll tell you how it was. When he
should have locked with both his hilts, he in a bravery
flourished over his head. With that comes Franklin at him
lustily and hurts the slave; with that he slinks away. Now his   55
way had been to have come in hand and feet, one and two
round at his costard. He like a fool bears his sword-point half a
yard out of danger. I lie here for my life. [*He takes up a position
of defence.*] If the devil come and he have no more strength
than fence, he shall never beat me from this ward; I'll stand to it.   60
A buckler in a skilful hand is as good as a castle; nay, 'tis better

---

45 *lay it on* provide generous hospitality
46 *and* if
    bid invite
50 *long of* on account of
53 *locked* attacked, crossed swords
    hilts The hilt of a sword being divided in three parts—pommel, handle, and shell—could
    be spoken of as plural (eg., *1 Henry IV,* II.iv, 202). Here, however, it probably refers to
    Shakebag's sword and dagger.
    in a bravery with a show of bravado
56 *in* ed. (not in Qq)
    come in 'to make a pass or home thrust, to get within the opponent's guard' (see *1 Henry
    IV,* II.iv, 209–10)
57 *round* directly
    costard head (really an apple, but often applied humorously or derisively to the head)
60 *fence* fencing skill
    ward defensive posture
60–1 *I'll stand to it* i.e., 'I'll fight fiercely to maintain it'. Punctuated differently, so that it
    becomes part of the next sentence, the phrase would mean 'I'll maintain that'. See Wine,
    who punctuates in this alternative way.
61 *buckler* small round shield

than a sconce, for I have tried it. Mosby, perceiving this, began
to faint. With that comes Arden with his arming-sword and
thrust him through the shoulder in a trice.

ALICE

Ay, but I wonder why you both stood still.   65

BLACK WILL

Faith, I was so amazed I could not strike.

ALICE

Ah, sirs, had he yesternight been slain,
For every drop of his detested blood
I would have crammed in angels in thy fist.
And kissed thee, too, and hugged thee in my arms.   70

BLACK WILL

Patient yourself; we cannot help it now.
Greene and we two will dog him through the fair,
And stab him in the crowd, and steal away.

Here enters MOSBY [*his arm bandaged*]

ALICE

It is unpossible. But here comes he
That will, I hope, invent some surer means.   75
Sweet Mosby, hide thy arm; it kills my heart.

MOSBY

Ay, Mistress Arden, this is your favour.

ALICE

Ah, say not so; for when I saw thee hurt
I could have took the weapon thou let'st fall
And run at Arden, for I have sworn   80
That these mine eyes, offended with his sight,
Shall never close till Arden's be shut up.

---

62 *sconce* small fort
   this i.e., Shakebag's injury and defeat.
63 *faint* lose heart or courage
   arming-sword sometimes glossed as 'broad sword', but more likely 'the sword with which
   he was armed'. See *O.E.D.* 1.b., 'Forming part of arms or armour'.
69 *have crammed in angels* Q3 (cramme in Angels Q1; have camd in angels Q2)
71 *Patient yourself* Calm yourself, be patient
77 *favour* a gift 'given to a lover ... to be worn conspicuously as a token of affection'
   (*O.E.D.*, sb.,7).

This night I rose and walked about the chamber,
And twice or thrice I thought to have murdered him.

MOSBY

What, in the night? Then had we been undone!   85

ALICE

Why, how long shall he live?

MOSBY

Faith, Alice, no longer than this night.
Black Will and Shakebag, will you two
Perform the complot that I have laid?

BLACK WILL

Ay, or else think me as a villain.   90

GREENE

And rather than you shall want, I'll help myself.

MOSBY

You, Master Greene, shall single Franklin forth
And hold him with a long tale of strange news,
That he may not come home till suppertime.
I'll fetch Master Arden home, and we, like friends,   95
Will play a game or two at tables here.

ALICE

But what of all this? How shall he be slain?

MOSBY

Why, Black Will and Shakebag, locked within the
    countinghouse,
Shall, at a certain watchword given, rush forth.

BLACK WILL

What shall the watchword be?   100

MOSBY

'Now I take you' — that shall be the word.
But come not forth before in any case.

BLACK WILL

I warrant you; but who shall lock me in?

ALICE

That will I do; thou'st keep the key thyself.

83 *This night* i.e. last night
91 *want* fail (*O.E.D.*, v.I.†d)
96 *tables* backgammon
98 *countinghouse* private room used as an office

MOSBY

> Come, Master Greene, go you along with me. 105
> See all things ready, Alice, against we come.

ALICE

> Take no care for that; send you him home.

Exeunt MOSBY *and* GREENE

> And if he e'er go forth again blame me.
> Come, Black Will, that in mine eyes art fair;
> Next unto Mosby do I honour thee. 110
> Instead of fair words and large promises
> My hands shall play you golden harmony.
> How like you this? Say, will you do it, sirs?

BLACK WILL

> Ay, and that bravely, too. Mark my device:
> Place Mosby, being a stranger, in a chair, 115
> And let your husband sit upon a stool,
> That I may come behind him cunningly
> And with a towel pull him to the ground,
> Then stab him till his flesh be as a sieve.
> That done, bear him behind the Abbey, 120
> That those that find him murdered may suppose
> Some slave or other killed him for his gold.

ALICE

> A fine device! You shall have twenty pound,
> And when he is dead you shall have forty more.
> And lest you might be suspected staying here, 125
> Michael shall saddle you two lusty geldings.
> Ride whither you will, to Scotland or to Wales,
> I'll see you shall not lack where'er you be.

---

106 *against* by the time that, before

107 *Take . . . that* don't worry about that, leave that to me

112 *My . . . harmony* i.e., 'I'll give you gold crowns.' (See III.86–9.)

114 *bravely* excellently, splendidly

115–16 Wine quotes M. Jourdain, *English Decoration and Furniture of the Early Renaissance* (1500–1650), 1924, p. 241: 'This scarcity of chairs is due to their rarity during the early Renaissance. Stools and forms outnumbered the chairs in hall and parlour until the Restoration. . . . In domestic use the chair was the rightful seat of the master of the house, only given up by courtesy.' (See below, l. 284.)

119 *sieve* Q2 (siue) Q3 (sive) (sine Q1)

BLACK WILL

Such words would make one kill a thousand men!
Give me the key; which is the countinghouse?   130

ALICE

Here would I stay and still encourage you,
But that I know how resolute you are.

SHAKEBAG

Tush! You are too faint-hearted; we must do it.

ALICE

But Mosby will be there, whose very, looks
Will add unwonted courage to my thought,   135
And make me the first that shall adventure on him.

BLACK WILL

Tush, get you gone; 'tis we must do the deed.
When this door opens next, look for his death.

                    [*Exeunt* BLACK WILL *and* SHAKEBAG]

ALICE

Ah, would he now were here, that it might open.
I shall no more be closed in Arden's arms,   140
That like the snakes of black Tisiphone
Sting me with their embracings. Mosby's arms
Shall compass me, and, were I made a star,
I would have none other spheres but those.
There is no nectar but in Mosby's lips!   145
Had chaste Diana kissed him, she like me
Would grow love-sick, and from her wat'ry bower
Fling down Endymion and snatch him up.
Then blame not me that slay a silly man
Not half so lovely as Endymion.   150

                    Here enters MICHAEL

MICHAEL

Mistress, my master is coming hard by.

136 *adventure on* attack
139–50 This speech, with its ironic and hyperbolic comparisons, reveals strikingly the widening gap between Alice's own perceptions of her actions and their real nature. (See also Ousby, p. 52.)
141 *Tisiphone* One of the Furies who pursued those who committed crimes against their kin. Their hair and arms were encircled with snakes, and each carried a torch and a whip to sting the consciences of the guilty.
142 *embracings* Q2–3 (enbraceings Q1)
148 *Endymion* A beautiful mortal with whom Diana, the goddess of the moon, fell in love.
    snatch Q2–3 (snath Q1)

ALICE

    Who comes with him?

MICHAEL

    Nobody but Mosby.

ALICE

    That's well, Michael. Fetch in the tables; and, when thou hast
    done, stand before the countinghouse door.   155

MICHAEL

    Why so?

ALICE

    Black Will is locked within to do the deed.

MICHAEL

    What, shall he die tonight?

ALICE

    Ay, Michael.

MICHAEL   160

    But shall not Susan know it?

ALICE

    Yes, for she'll be as secret as ourselves.

MICHAEL

    That's brave! I'll go fetch the tables.

ALICE

    But Michael, hark to me a word or two:
    When my husband is come in, lock the street door;
    He shall be murdered ere the guests come in.   165
                      Exit MICHAEL [*and re-enter with the tables*]

Here enters ARDEN *and* MOSBY

    Husband, what mean you to bring Mosby home?
    Although I wished you to be reconciled,
    'Twas more for fear of you than love of him.
    Black Will and Greene are his companions,

---

162 *brave* splendid
165 *ere* Q3 (or Q1–2) before
168 *of you* i.e. for you
169 *Greene* One would, as Sturgess observes, 'expect "Shakebag", not "Greene", at this
    point. Greene is not a "cutter", and it was Shakebag, not Greene, involved with Mosby
    and Black Will in the scuffle of Scene XIII.' Sturgess points out that 'Greene' suits the
    rhythm of the line better, but, I suggest, it may well be a dangerous slip on Alice's part
    that momentarily chills the hearts of her accomplices.

And they are cutters and may cut you short;   170
Therefore, I thought it good to make you friends.
But wherefore do you bring him hither now?
You have given me my supper with his sight.
MOSBY

Master Arden, methinks your wife would have me gone.
ARDEN

No, good Master Mosby, women will be prating.   175
Alice, bid him welcome; he and I are friends.
ALICE

You may enforce me to it if you will,
But I had rather die than bid him welcome.
His company hath purchased me ill friends,
And therefore will I ne'er frequent it more.   180
MOSBY

[*Aside*] Oh, how cunningly she can dissemble!
ARDEN

Now he is here, you will not serve me so.
ALICE

I pray you be not angry or displeased;
I'll bid him welcome, seeing you'll have it so:
You are welcome, Master Mosby. Will you sit down?   185
MOSBY

I know I am welcome to your loving husband,
But for yourself you speak not from your heart.
ALICE

And if I do not, sir, think I have cause.
MOSBY

Pardon me, Master Arden, I'll away.
ARDEN

No, good Master Mosby.   190
ALICE

We shall have guests enough though you go hence.
MOSBY

I pray you, Master Arden, let me go.
ARDEN

I pray thee, Mosby, let her prate her fill.
ALICE

The doors are open, sir; you may be gone.

189 *Master* ed. (M. Q1–2; mistris Q3)

MICHAEL

    [*Aside*] Nay, that's a lie, for I have locked the doors.   195

ARDEN

    Sirrah, fetch me a cup of wine; I'll make them friends.

                          [*Exit* MICHAEL]

    And, gentle Mistress Alice, seeing you are so stout,

    You shall begin. Frown not; I'll have it so.

ALICE

    I pray you meddle with that you have to do.

ARDEN

    Why, Alice, how can I do too much for him   200

    Whose life I have endangered without cause?

              [*Enter* MICHAEL *with wine*]

ALICE

    'Tis true; and seeing 'twas partly through my means,

    I am content to drink to him for this once.

    Here, Master Mosby! And, I pray you, henceforth

    Be you as strange to me as I to you.   205

    Your company hath purchased me ill friends,

    And I for you, God knows, have undeserved

    Been ill spoken of in every place;

    Therefore, henceforth frequent my house no more.

MOSBY

    I'll see your husband in despite of you.   210

    Yet, Arden, I protest to thee by heaven,

    Thou ne'er shalt see me more after this night.

    I'll go to Rome rather than be forsworn.

ARDEN

    Tush, I'll have no such vows made in my house.

ALICE

    Yes, I pray you, husband, let him swear;   215

    And on that condition, Mosby, pledge me here.

---

195 Michael, who exited at l. 165, must re-enter at some point before his line.
197 *stout* stubborn
198 *begin* i.e. make the first toast
216 *pledge* drink to

MOSBY

    Ay, as willingly as I mean to live.

ARDEN

    Come, Alice, is our supper ready yet?

ALICE

    It will by then you have played a game at tables.

ARDEN

    Come, Master Mosby, what shall we play for?   220

MOSBY

    Three games for a French crown, sir, and please you.

ARDEN

    Content.

Then they play at the tables
[*Enter* BLACK WILL *and* SHAKEBAG]

BLACK WILL

    [*Aside*] Can he not take him yet? What a spite is that!

ALICE

    [*Aside*] Not yet, Will. Take heed he see thee not.

BLACK WILL

    [*Aside*] I fear he will spy me as I am coming.   225

MICHAEL

    [*Aside*] To prevent that, creep betwixt my legs.

MOSBY

    One ace, or else I lose the game.   [*He throws the dice*]

ARDEN

    Marry, sir, there's two for failing.

MOSBY

    Ah, Master Arden, 'Now I can take you.'

          Then [BLACK] WILL *pulls him down with a towel*

ARDEN

    Mosby! Michael! Alice! What will you do?   230

BLACK WILL

    Nothing but take you up, sir, nothing else.

227 *ace* side of the dice marked with a single dot
228 *for failing* i.e., 'in case one is not enough' (see *for*, I.225).
231 *take you up* deal with you (playing on the 'watchword').

MOSBY

There's for the pressing iron you told me of.

[*He hits him with the iron*]

SHAKEBAG

And there's for the ten pound in my sleeve.

[*Stabs him*]

ALICE

What, groans thou? Nay then, give me the weapon.
Take this for hind'ring Mosby's love and mine.   235

[*Stabs him*]

MICHAEL

Oh, Mistress!

[ARDEN *dies*]

BLACK WILL

Ah, that villain will betray us all.

MOSBY

Tush, fear him not; he will be secret.

MICHAEL

Why, dost thou think I will betray myself?

SHAKEBAG   240

In Southwark dwells a bonny northern lass,
The widow Chambley; I'll to her house now,
And if she will not give me harborough,
I'll make booty of the quean, even to her smock.

BLACK WILL

Shift for yourselves; we two will leave you now.

ALICE   245

First lay the body in the countinghouse.

Then they lay the body in the countinghouse

BLACK WILL

We have our gold. Mistress Alice, adieu;
Mosby, farewell, and Michael, farewell too.

Exeunt [BLACK WILL *and* SHAKEBAG]

232 In Holinshed, Mosby 'hauing at his girdle a pressing iron of fourteen pounds weight,
stroke him on the hed with the same, so that he fell downe, and gaue a great grone,
insomuch that they thought he had beene killed.' The playwright picks up the 'grone' at
l. 234, so perhaps he also intended that Mosby should kill Arden with an iron. There is
no stage direction in Qq.
234 *the weapon* presumably Shakebag's sword or dagger.
240 *Southwark* 'A borough, formerly independent of the London city government,' where
most of the playhouses were erected (the Globe, the Rose, the Swan, etc.) as well as the
bear-baiting ring at Paris Garden (Sugden).
242 *harborough* harbour, shelter
243 *quean* strumpet, harlot

Enter SUSAN

SUSAN

Mistress, the guests are at the doors.

Hearken, they knock. What, shall I let them in?

ALICE

Mosby, go thou and bear them company.   250

Exit MOSBY

And, Susan, fetch water and wash away this blood.

[*Exit* SUSAN, *returns with water, and washes the floor*]

SUSAN

The blood cleaveth to the ground and will not out.

ALICE

But with my nails I'll scrape away the blood.

The more I strive the more the blood appears!

SUSAN

What's the reason, Mistress, can you tell?   255

ALICE

Because I blush not at my husband's death.

Here enters MOSBY

MOSBY

How now, what's the matter? Is all well?

ALICE

Ay, well, if Arden were alive again!

In vain we strive, for here his blood remains.

MOSBY

Why, strew rushes on it, can you not?   260

This wench doth nothing; fall unto the work.

ALICE

'Twas thou that made me murder him.

MOSBY   What of that?

ALICE

Nay, nothing, Mosby, so it be not known.

251–4 *And, Susan . . . appears* Cf. *Macbeth*, II.ii, 59–60: 'Will all great Neptune's ocean wash this blood/Clean from my hand?'

260 *rushes* 'Down to the seventeenth century green rushes were commonly employed for strewing on the floors' (*O.E.D*,).

MOSBY

Keep thou it close, and 'tis unpossible.

ALICE

Ah, but I cannot. Was he not slain by me? 265
My husband's death torments me at the heart.

MOSBY

It shall not long torment thee, gentle Alice,
I am thy husband; think no more on him.

Here enters ADAM FOWLE *and* BRADSHAW

BRADSHAW

How now, Mistress Arden, what ail you weep?

MOSBY

Because her husband is abroad so late. 270
A couple of ruffians threat'ned him yesternight,
And she, poor soul, is afraid he should be hurt.

ADAM

Is't nothing else? Tush, he'll be here anon.

Here enters GREENE

GREENE

Now, Mistress Arden, lack you any guests?

ALICE

Ah, Master Greene, did you see my husband lately? 275

GREENE

I saw him walking behind the Abbey even now.

Here enters FRANKLIN

ALICE

I do not like this being out so late.
Master Franklin, where did you leave my husband?

FRANKLIN

Believe me, I saw him not since morning.
Fear you not, he'll come anon. Meantime, 280
You may do well to bid his guests sit down.

ALICE

Ay, so they shall. Master Bradshaw, sit you there;

264 *close* secret

I pray you be content, I'll have my will.
Master Mosby, sit you in my husband's seat.

MICHAEL

[*Aside*] Susan, shall thou and I wait on them?   285
Or, and thou say'st the word, let us sit down too.

SUSAN

[*Aside*] Peace, we have other matters now in hand.
I fear me, Michael, all will be bewrayed.

MICHAEL

[*Aside*] Tush, so it be known that I shall marry thee in the
morning I care not though I be hanged ere night. But to prevent   290
the worst I'll buy some ratsbane.

SUSAN

[*Aside*] Why, Michael, wilt thou poison thyself?

MICHAEL

[*Aside*] No, but my mistress, for I fear she'll tell,

SUSAN

[*Aside*] Tush, Michael, fear not her; she's wise enough.

MOSBY

Sirrah Michael, give's a cup of beer.   295
Mistress Arden, here's to your husband.

ALICE

My husband!

FRANKLIN

What ails you, woman, to cry so suddenly?

ALICE

Ah, neighbours, a sudden qualm came over my heart;
My husband's being forth torments my mind.   300
I know something's amiss; he is not well,
Or else I should have heard of him ere now.

MOSBY

[*Aside*] She will undo us through her foolishness.

GREENE

Fear not, Mistress Arden, he's well enough.

ALICE

Tell not me; I know he is not well.   305
He was not wont for to stay thus late.
Good Master Franklin, go and seek him forth,

288 *bewrayed* betrayed, revealed
291 *ratsbane* rat poison, arsenic

101

And if you find him send him home to me,
And tell him what a fear he hath put me in.

FRANKLIN
[*Aside*] I like not this; I pray God all be well.—   310
I'll seek him out and find him if I can.

Exeunt FRANKLIN, MOSBY, *and* GREENE

ALICE
[*Aside*] Michael, how shall I do to rid the rest away?

MICHAEL
[*Aside*] Leave that to my charge; let me alone.—
'Tis very late, Master Bradshaw,
And there are many false knaves abroad,   315
And you have many narrow lanes to pass.

BRADSHAW
Faith, friend Michael, and thou sayest true.
Therefore I pray thee light's forth and lend's a link.

Exeunt BRADSHAW, ADAM [FOWLE], *and* MICHAEL

ALICE
[*Aside*] Michael, bring them to the doors, but do not stay;
You know I do not love to be alone.—   320
Go, Susan, and bid thy brother come.
But wherefore should he come? Here is nought but fear.
Stay, Susan, stay, and help to counsel me.

SUSAN
Alas, I counsel! Fear frights away my wits.

Then they open the countinghouse door and look upon ARDEN

ALICE
See, Susan, where thy quondam master lies;   325
Sweet Arden, smeared in blood and filthy gore.

SUSAN
My brother, you, and I shall rue this deed.

ALICE
Come, Susan, help to lift his body forth.
And let our salt tears be his obsequies.

[*They lift his body out of the countinghouse*]

Here enters MOSBY *and* GREENE

311 s.d. after l. 310 in Qq
318 *link* torch
325 *quondam* former

MOSBY

How now, Alice, whither will you bear him? 330

ALICE

Sweet Mosby, art thou come? Then weep that will;
I have my wish in that I joy thy sight.

GREENE

Well, it 'hoves us to be circumspect.

MOSBY

Ay, for Franklin thinks that we have murdered him.

ALICE

Ay, but he cannot prove it for his life. 335
We'll spend this night in dalliance and in sport.

Here enters MICHAEL

MICHAEL

Oh mistress, the mayor and all the watch
Are coming towards our house with glaives and bills.

ALICE

Make the door fast; let them not come in.

MOSBY

Tell me, sweet Alice, how shall I escape? 340

ALICE

Out at the back door, over the pile of wood,
And for one night lie at the Flower-de-Luce.

MOSBY

That is the next way to betray myself.

GREENE

Alas, Mistress Arden, the watch will take me here,
And cause suspicion where else would be none. 345

ALICE

Why, take that way that Master Mosby doth;
But first convey the body to the fields.

MOSBY

Until tomorrow, sweet Alice; now farewell,
And see you confess nothing in any case.

333 *'hoves* behoves
338 *glaives* swords
    bills halberds
343 *next* quickest, surest

GREENE

    Be resolute, Mistress Alice; betray us not,   350

    But cleave to us as we will stick to you.

          Then they [MOSBY, GREENE, MICHAEL, *and* SUSAN]

                bear the body into the fields

ALICE

    Now let the judge and juries do their worst;

    My house is clear and now I fear them not.

             [*Enter* MICHAEL *and* SUSAN]

SUSAN

    As we went it snowed all the way,

    Which makes me fear our footsteps will be spied.   355

ALICE

    Peace, fool! The snow will cover them again.

SUSAN

    But it had done before we came back again.

ALICE

    Hark, hark, they knock! Go, Michael, let them in.

         [MICHAEL *opens the door*]

       Here enters the MAYOR *and the* WATCH

    How now, Master Mayor, have you brought my husband home?

MAYOR

    I saw him come into your house an hour ago.   360

ALICE

    You are deceived; it was a Londoner.

MAYOR

    Mistress Arden, know you not one that is called Black Will?

ALICE

    I know none such. What mean these questions?

---

351 s.d. Qq place the stage direction after l. 347, which means that Mosby and Greene
return merely to speak a total of 4 lines before they exit again. In performance it is more
practical if the exit is delayed until l. 351. Alice can then busy herself with straightening
the room ('My house is clear'), until Michael and Susan return on l. 353. Susan's
information is so important that it provides a good entry line.

357 *done* i.e. stopped snowing

361 *a Londoner* According to Holinshed, after the murder Alice 'sent for two Londoners to
supper, the one named Prune, and the other Cole, that were grosers'.

MAYOR

I have the Council's warrant to apprehend him.

ALICE

[*Aside*] I am glad it is no worse.—   365
Why, Master Mayor, think you I harbour any such?

MAYOR

We are informed that here he is,
And therefore pardon us, for we must search.

ALICE

Ay, search, and spare you not, through every room.
Were my husband at home you would not offer this.   370

Here enters FRANKLIN

Master Franklin, what mean you come so sad?

FRANKLIN

Arden, thy husband and my friend, is slain.

ALICE

Ah, by whom, Master Franklin? Can you tell?

FRANKLIN

I know not; but behind the Abbey
There he lies murdered in most piteous case.   375

MAYOR

But, Master Franklin, are you sure 'tis he?

FRANKLIN

I am too sure; would God I were deceived.

ALICE

Find out the murderers; let them be known.

FRANKLIN

Ay, so they shall. Come you along with us.

ALICE

Wherefore?   380

FRANKLIN

Know you this hand-towel and this knife?

SUSAN

[*Aside*] Ah, Michael, through this thy negligence
Thou hast betrayed and undone us all.

MICHAEL

[*Aside*] I was so afraid I knew not what I did.

375 *piteous case* pitiful condition

I thought I had thrown them both into the well.   385

ALICE

It is the pig's blood we had to supper.
But wherefore stay you? Find out the murderers.

MAYOR

I fear me you'll prove one of them yourself.

ALICE

I one of them? What mean such questions?

FRANKLIN

I fear me he was murdered in this house   390
And carried to the fields, for from that place
Backwards and forwards may you see
The print of many feet within the snow.
And look about this chamber where we are,
And you shall find part of his guiltless blood;   395
For in his slipshoe did I find some rushes,
Which argueth he was murdered in this room.

MAYOR

Look in the place where he was wont to sit.
See, see! His blood! It is too manifest.

ALICE   400

It is a cup of wine that Michael shed.

MICHAEL

Ay, truly.

FRANKLIN

It is his blood which, strumpet, thou hast shed.
But if I live, thou and thy complices
Which have conspired and wrought his death shall rue it.

ALICE   405

Ah, Master Franklin, God and heaven can tell
I loved him more than all the world beside.
But bring me to him; let me see his body.

FRANKLIN

Bring that villain and Mosby's sister too;
And one of you go to the Flower-de-Luce
And seek for Mosby, and apprehend him too.   410

Exeunt

386 *to* for
396 *slipshoe* slipper
408 *that villain* i.e., Michael.

SCENE XV

Here enters SHAKEBAG *solus*

SHAKEBAG

The widow Chambley in her husband's days I kept;
And now he's dead she is grown so stout
She will not know her old companions.
I came thither, thinking to have had
Harbour as I was wont,   5
And she was ready to thrust me out at doors.
But whether she would or no I got me up,
And as she followed me I spurned her down the stairs
And broke her neck, and cut her tapster's throat;
And now I am going to fling them in the Thames.   10
I have the gold; what care I though it be known?
I'll cross the water and take sanctuary.

Exit SHAKEBAG

---

0 *s.d solus* alone
1 *kept* i.e. as a mistress
2 *stout* proud
8 *spurned* kicked

12 *take sanctuary* i.e. seek refuge in one of the areas of a church or royal palace where criminals were safe from arrest for crimes other than blasphemy or treason. Wine points out that, according to XIV.240–1, if Shakebag has been to the widow Chambley's he is already in Southwark, where the Mint was designated a sanctuary, and where he is eventually murdered (see Epilogue, 3–5).

SCENE XVI

Here enters the MAYOR, MOSBY, ALICE, FRANKLIN, MICHAEL,
and SUSAN [*guarded by the* WATCH]

MAYOR

    See, Mistress Arden, where your husband lies.
    Confess this foul fault and be penitent.

ALICE

    Arden, sweet husband, what shall I say?
    The more I sound his name the more he bleeds.
    This blood condemns me, and in gushing forth   5
    Speaks as it falls and asks me why I did it.
    Forgive me, Arden; I repent me now;
    And would my death save thine thou shouldst not die.
    Rise up, sweet Arden, and enjoy thy love,
    And frown not on me when we meet in heaven;   10
    In heaven I love thee though on earth I did not.

MAYOR

    Say, Mosby, what made thee murder him?

FRANKLIN

    Study not for an answer, look not down.
    His purse and girdle found at thy bed's head
    Witness sufficiently thou didst the deed.   15
    It bootless is to swear thou didst it not.

MOSBY

    I hired Black Will and Shakebag, ruffians both,
    And they and I have done this murd'rous deed.
    But wherefore stay we? Come and bear me hence.

4–6 *The more ... did it* It was popularly believed that the corpse of a murdered man bled
in the presence of his killer. Cf. *Richard III*, I.ii, 55–61.

13 *study not* do not try to invent

14 *girdle* belt (to carry the purse)

16 *bootless* useless, pointless

17–19 Sturgess points out that it was, in fact, Greene who did the hiring at Alice's suggestion
and with her money, and he suggests that this claim by Mosby is 'either an error of the
playwright or a device by the playwright to cover Greene's absence.' As Wine observes,
however, Mosby's confession 'stems from a desperate awareness that the game is up. l. 19
makes it obvious that he wants the whole affair quickly over with.' He displays the same
attitude in Scene XVIII (see l. 13 and l. 35).

FRANKLIN

    Those ruffians shall not escape. I will up to London   20
    And get the Council's warrant to apprehend them.

                                          Exeunt

SCENE XVII

Here enters [BLACK] WILL

BLACK WILL

    Shakebag, I hear, hath taken sanctuary;
    But I am so pursued with hues and cries
    For petty robberies that I have done
    That I can come unto no sanctuary.
    Therefore must I in some oyster-boat   5
    At last be fain to go aboard some hoy,
    And so to Flushing. There is no staying here.
    At Sittingburgh the watch was like to take me,
    And, had I not with my buckler covered my head
    And run full blank at all adventures,   10
    I am sure I had ne'er gone further than that place,
    For the constable had twenty warrants to apprehend me;
    Besides that, I robbed him and his man once at Gadshill.
    Farewell, England; I'll to Flushing now.

                            Exit [BLACK] WILL

---

6 *hoy* small boat used to carry passengers and goods
8 *like* likely
10 *full . . . adventures* headlong whatever the outcome
13 *Gadshill* 'A hill on the road from London to Rochester' (Sugden). The scene of Falstaff s famous encounter with the 'rogues in buckram' (*1 Henry IV,* II.iv.). See also VII.18n., above.

SCENE XVIII

Here enters the MAYOR, MOSBY, ALICE, MICHAEL,
SUSAN, *and* BRADSHAW [*and the* WATCH]

MAYOR
    Come, make haste, and bring away the prisoners.

BRADSHAW
    Mistress Arden, you are now going to God,
    And I am by the law condemned to die
    About a letter I brought from Master Greene.
    I pray you, Mistress Arden, speak the truth: 5
    Was I ever privy to your intent or no?

ALICE
    What should I say? You brought me such a letter,
    But I dare swear thou knewest not the contents.
    Leave now to trouble me with worldly things,
    And let me meditate upon my Saviour Christ,   10
    Whose blood must save me for the blood I shed.

MOSBY
    How long shall I live in this hell of grief?
    Convey me from the presence of that strumpet.

ALICE
    Ah, but for thee I had never been strumpet.
    What cannot oaths and protestations do   15
    When men have opportunity to woo?
    I was too young to sound thy villainies,
    But now I find it, and repent too late.

SUSAN
    Ah, gentle brother, wherefore should I die?
    I knew not of it till the deed was done.   20

---

 4 *About* On account of
 5–7 *I pray . . . a letter* Faversham was renowned for its oyster beds, particularly by the Dutch,
    who traded regularly with the town.
 6 *privy to* aware of
 9 *Leave* Cease
17 *sound* fathom

MOSBY

    For thee I mourn more than for myself,
    But let it suffice I cannot save thee now.

MICHAEL

    And if your brother and my mistress
    Had not promised me you in marriage,
    I had ne'er given consent to this foul deed.   25

MAYOR

    Leave to accuse each other now,
    And listen to the sentence I shall give:
    Bear Mosby and his sister to London straight,
    Where they in Smithfield must be executed;
    Bear Mistress Arden unto Canterbury,   30
    Where her sentence is she must be burnt;
    Michael and Bradshaw in Faversham must suffer death.

ALICE

    Let my death make amends for all my sins.

MOSBY

    Fie upon women! — this shall be my song.
    But bear me hence, for I have lived too long.   35

SUSAN

    Seeing no hope on earth, in heaven is my hope.

MICHAEL

    Faith, I care not, seeing I die with Susan.

BRADSHAW

    My blood be on his head that gave the sentence!

MAYOR

    To speedy execution with them all!

                                      Exeunt

28 *straight* immediately
29 *Smithfield* 'An open space, East of the Tower of London just outside the city walls. It was a haunt of riverside thieves, and was often used as the place for their execution' (Sugden).

EPILOGUE

Here enters FRANKLIN

FRANKLIN
Thus have you seen the truth of Arden's death.
As for the ruffians, Shakebag and Black Will,
The one took sanctuary, and being sent for out,
Was murdered in Southwark as he passed
To Greenwich where the Lord Protector lay.   5
Black Will was burnt in Flushing on a stage;
Greene was hanged at Osbridge n Kent;
The painter fled, and how he died we know not.
But this above the rest is to be noted:
Arden lay murdered in that plot of ground   10
Which he by force and violence held from Reede;
And in the grass his body's print was seen
Two years and more after the deed was done.
Gentlemen, we hope you'll pardon this naked tragedy,
Wherein no filed points are foisted in   15
To make it gracious to the ear or eye;
For simple truth is gracious enough,
And needs no other points of glozing stuff.   [*Exit*]

6 *stage* scaffold
7 *Osbridge* i.e., Ospringe, 'a village in Kent, a mile or so South-West of Faversham'
(Sugden).
14 *naked* plain, straightforward
15 *filed points* rhetorical figures. See Ousby for the view that far from being 'wholly con-
ventional' or a 'mere formula', the 'playwright is warning us that rather than functioning
as graceful adornment, "filed points" can be as deadly as dagger points.'
18 *glozing* specious

112

APPENDIX

From Holinshed's *Chronicles of England, Scotland and Ireland*

(Second Edition, 1587, 3 vols in 2, Vol. III, pp. 1062–1066).

1551
Anno Reg. 5.

Arden murdered.

Arden described.

Love and lust.

A pair of silver dice work much mischief.

Arden winketh at his wife's lewdness, and why!

Arden's wife attempteth means to make away her husband.

About this time there was, at Faversham in Kent, a gentleman named Arden most cruelly murdered and slain by the procurement of his own wife. The which murder, for the horribleness thereof (although otherwise it may seem to be but a private matter, and therefore, as it were, impertinent to this history), I have thought good to set it forth somewhat at large, having the instructions delivered to me by them that used some diligence to gather the true understanding of the circumstances. This Arden was a man of a tall and comely personage, and matched in marriage with a gentle-woman young, tall and well favoured of shape and countenance, who chancing to fall in familiarity with one Mosby (a tailor by occupation, a black swart man, servant to the Lord North), it happened this Mosby, upon some misliking, to fall out with her. But she, being desirous to be in favour with him again, sent him a pair of silver dice by one Adam Fowle, dwelling at the Flower-de-Luce in Faversham.

After which he resorted to her again, and oftentimes lay in Arden's house, insomuch that within two years after he obtained such favour at her hands that he lay with her, or, as they term it, kept her, in abusing her body. And although (as it was said), Master Arden perceived right well their mutual familiarity to be much greater than their honesty, yet because he would not offend her and so lose the benefit which he hoped to gain at some of her friends hands in bearing with her lewdness, which he might have lost if he should have fallen out with her, he was contented to wink at her filthy disorder, and both permitted and also invited Mosby very often to ie in his house. And thus it continued a good space before any practice was begun by them against Master Arden. She, at length, inflamed in love with Mosby, and loathing her husband, wished and after practised the means how to hasten his end.

There was a painter dwelling in Faversham who had skill of poisons, as was reported. She therefore demanded of him whether it were true that he had such skill in that feat or not, and he denied not but that he had indeed. 'Yea,' said she, 'but I would have such a one made as should have most vehement

113

and speedy operation to dispatch the eater thereof.' 'That can I do,' quoth he, and forthwith made her such a one, and willed her to put it into the bottom of a porringer and then after to pour milk on it; which circumstance she forgetting, did clean contrary, putting in the milk first, and afterward the poison. Now Master Arden purposing that day to ride to Canterbury, his wife brought him his breakfast, which was wont to be milk and butter. He, having received a spoonful or two of the milk, misliked the taste and colour thereof, and said to his wife, 'Mistress Alice, what milk have you given me here?' Wherewithal she tilted it over with her hand, saying, 'I ween nothing can please you.' Then he took horse and rode to Canterbury, and by the way fell into extreme purging upwards and downwards, and so escaped for that time.

Arden is poisoned by his wife but recovereth.

After this, his wife fell in acquaintance with one Greene of Faversham, from which Greene Master Arden had wrested a piece of ground on the backside of the Abbey of Faversham, and there had blows and great threats passed betwixt them about that matter. Therefore she, knowing that Greene hated her husband, began to practise with him how to make him away, and concluded that if he could get any that that would kill him, he should have ten pounds for a reward. This Greene, having doings for his master—Sir Anthony Ager—had occasion to go up to London where his master then lay, and having some charge up with him, desired one Bradshaw, a goldsmith of Faversham that was his neighbour, to accompany him to Gravesend, and he would content him for his pains. This Bradshaw, being a very honest man, was content, and rode with him. And when they came to Rainham Down they chanced to see three or four servingmen that were coming from Leeds, and therewith Bradshaw espied coming up the hill from Rochester one Black Will, a terrible cruel ruffian with a sword and buckler, and another with a great staff on his neck.

She deviseth another way to dispatch her husband Arden.

A notorious murdering ruffian.

Then said Bradshaw to Greene, 'We are happy that here cometh some company from Leeds, for here cometh up against us as murdering a knave as any is in England. If it were not for them we might chance hardly to escape without loss of our money and lives.' 'Yea,' thought Greene, as he after confessed, 'such a one is for my purpose,' and therefore asked, 'Which is he?' 'Yonder is he,' quoth Bradshaw, 'the same that hath the sword and buckler: his name is Black Will.' 'How know you that?' said Greene. Bradshaw answered, 'I knew him at Boulogne, where we both served. He was a soldier, and I was Sir Richard Cavendish's man, and there he

Mark how the devil will not let his organs or instruments let slip either occasion or opportunity to commit most heinous wickedness.

committed many robberies and heinous murders on such as travelled betwixt Boulogne and France.'

By this time the other company of servingmen came to them, and they all going together met with Black Will and his fellow. The servingmen knew Black Will and, saluting him, demanded of him whither he went. He answered, 'By His blood!' (for his use was to swear almost at every word), 'I know not, nor care not, but set up my staff, and even as it falleth I go.' 'If thou,' quoth they, 'wilt go back again to Gravesend, we will give thee thy supper.' 'By His blood!' said he, 'I care not. I am content; have with you.' And so he returned again with them. Then Black Will took acquaintance of Bradshaw, saying, 'Fellow Bradshaw, how dost thou?' Bradshaw, unwilling to renew acquaintance or to have aught to do with so shameless a ruffian, said, 'Why, do ye know me?' 'Yea, that I do,' quoth he. 'Did not we serve in Boulogne together?' 'But ye must pardon me,' quoth Bradshaw, 'for I have forgotten you.'

Then Greene talked with Black Will, and said, 'When ye have supped, come to mine host's house at such a sign and I will give you the sack and sugar.' 'By His blood!' said he, 'I thank you. I will come and take it I warrant you.' According to his promise he came, and there they made good cheer. Then Black Will and Greene went and talked apart from Bradshaw, and there concluded together that if he would kill Master Arden he should have ten pounds for his labour. Then he answered, 'By His wounds! That I will if I may know him.' 'Marry, tomorrow in Paul's I will show him thee,' said Greene. Then they left their talk, and Greene bade him go home to his host's house. Then Greene wrote a letter to Mistress Arden, and among other things put in these words: 'We have got a man for our purpose; we may thank my brother Bradshaw'. Now Bradshaw, not knowing anything of this, took the letter of him, and in the morning departed home again, and delivered the letter to Mistress Arden. And Greene and Black Will went up to London at the tide.

At the time appointed, Greene showed Black Will Master Arden walking in Paul's. Then said Black Will, 'What is he that goeth after him?' 'Marry,' said Greene, 'one of his men.' 'By His blood!' said Black Will, 'I will kill them both.' 'Nay,' said Greene, 'do not so, for he is of counsel with us in this matter.' 'By His blood,' said he, 'I care not for that, I will kill them both.' 'Nay,' said Greene, 'in any wise do not so.' Then Black Will thought to have killed Master Arden in Paul's

A desperate villain.

An honest man is ashamed to renew old acquaintance with a knave.

The match made to murder Arden.

Simplicity abused.

Black Will maketh no conscience of bloodshed and murder.

churchyard, but there were so many gentlemen that accompanied him to dinner that he missed of his purpose. Greene showed all this talk to Master Arden's man, whose name was Michael, which ever after stood in doubt of Black Will lest he should kill him. The cause that this Michael conspired with the rest against his master was for that it was determined that he should marry a kinswoman of Mosby's.

Why Arden's man conspired with the rest to kill his master.

After this, Master Arden lay at a certain parsonage which he held in London, and therefore his man Michael and Greene agreed that Black Will should come in the night to the parsonage, where he should find the doors left open that he might come in and murder Master Arden. This Michael, having his master to bed, left open the doors according to the appointment. His master, then being in bed, asked him if he had shut fast the doors, and he said, 'Yea.' But yet, afterwards, fearing lest Black Will would kill him as well as his master, after he was in bed himself, he rose again and shut the doors, bolting them fast, so that Black Will will coming thither and finding the doors shut, departed, being disappointed at that time. The next day, Black Will came to Greene in a great chafe, swearing and staring because he was so deceived, and with many terrible oaths threatened to kill Master Arden's man first, wheresoever he met him. 'No,' said Greene, 'do not so. I will first know the cause of shutting the doors.'

One murdering mind mistrusting another do hinder the action where about they agreed.

Then Greene met and talked with Arden's man, and asked of him why he did not leave open the doors according to his promise. 'Marry,' said Michael, 'I will show you the cause. My master yesternight did that he never did before, for after I was in bed he rose up and shut the doors, and in the morning rated me for leaving them unshut.' And herewith Greene and Black Will were pacified. Arden being ready to go homewards, his maid came to Greene and said, 'This night will my master go down.' Whereupon it was agreed that Black Will should kill him on Rainham Down. When Master Arden came to Rochester his man, still fearing that Black Will would kill him with his master, pricked his horse of purpose and made him to halt, to the end he might protract the time and tarry behind. His master asked him why his horse halted. He said, 'I know not.' 'Well,' quoth his master, 'when ye come at the smith here before, between Rochester and the hill-foot over against Cheetham, remove his shoe and search him, and then come after me.' So Master Arden rode on, and ere he came at the place where Black Will lay in wait for him there overtook him diverse gentlemen of his acquaintance who kept him company, so that Black Will missed here also of

The fourth attempt to make Arden away disappointed.

Black Will misseth his purpose.

116

his purpose.

After that Master Arden was come home, he sent, as he usually did, his man to Sheppey, to Sir Thomas Cheiny, then Lord Warden of the Cinque Ports, about certain business, and at his coming away he had a letter delivered sent by Sir Thomas Cheiny to his master. When he came home, his mistress took the letter and kept it, willing her man to tell his master that he had a letter delivered him by Sir Thomas Cheiny and that he had lost it, adding that he thought it best that his master should go the next morning to Sir Thomas, because he knew not the matter. He said he would, and therefore he willed his man to be stirring betimes. In this meanwhile, Black Will and one George Shakebag, his companion, were kept in a store-house of Sir Anthony Ager's at Preston by Greene's appointment, and thither came Mistress Arden to see him, bringing and sending him meat and drink many times. He, therefore, lurking there and watching some opportunity for his purpose, was willed in any wise to be up early in the morning to lie in wait for Master Arden in a certain broom close betwixt Faversham and the ferry (which close he needs must pass), there to do his feat. Now Black Will stirred in the morning betimes, but missed the way and tarried in a wrong place.

Arden's wife visiteth, succoureth, emboldeneth, and directeth Black Will, how to accomplish his bloody purpose.

Master Arden and his man coming on their way early in the morning towards Shorlow, where Sir Thomas Cheiny lay, as they were almost come to the broom close, his man, always fearing that Black Will would kill him with his master, feigned that he had lost his purse. 'Why,' said his master, 'thou foolish knave, couldst thou not look to thy purse but lose it? What was in it?' 'Three pounds,' said he. 'Why then, go thy ways back again like a knave,' said his master, 'and seek it, for being so early as it is there is no man stirring, and therefore thou mayest be sure to find it, and then come and overtake me at the ferry.' But nevertheless, by reason that Black Will lost his way, Master Arden escaped once again. At that time, Black Will yet thought he should have been sure to have met him homewards, but whether that some of the Lord Warden's men accompanied him back to Faversham, or that being in doubt, for that it was late to go through the broom close, and therefore took another way, Black Will was disappointed then also.

Note here the force of fear and a troubled conscience.

Black Will yet again disappointed.

But now Saint Valentine's fair being at hand, the conspirators thought to dispatch their devilish intention at that time. Mosby minded to pick some quarrel to Master Arden at the fair to fight with him, for, he said, he could not find it in his

A prepensed quarrel against

117

Arden by the conspirators.

heart to murder a gentleman in that sort as his wife wished, although she had made a solemn promise to him, and he again to her, to be in all points as man and wife together, and thereupon they both received the sacrament on a Sunday at London, openly in a church there. But this device to fight with him would not serve, for Master Arden, both then and at other times, had been greatly provoked by Mosby to fight with him, but he would not. Now Mosby had a sister that

Arden's wife Black Will , & the knot of villains meet and conclude upon their former prepensed mischief.

dwelt in a tenement of Master Arden's, near to his house in Faversham, and on the fair even, Black Will was sent for to come thither: and Greene bringing him thither met there with Mistress Arden, accompanied with Michael, her man, and one of her maids. There were also Mosby and George Shakebag, and there they devised to have killed him in manner as afterwards he was. But yet Mosby at the first would not agree to that cowardly murdering of him, but in a fury flung away, and went up the Abbey street towards the Flower-de-Luce, the house of the aforenamed Adam Fowle, where he did often host. But before he came thither, now at this time, a messenger overtook him that was sent from Mistress Arden, desiring him of all loves to come back again to help to accomplish the matter he knew of. Hereupon he returned to her

O Importunate & bloody minded strumpet!

again, and at his coming back she fell down upon her knees to him and besought him to go through with the matter, as if he loved her he would be content to do; sith, as she had divers times told him, he needed not to doubt, for there was not any that would care for his death, nor make any great enquiry for them that should dispatch him.

Thus, she being earnest with him, at length he was contented to agree unto that horrible device, and thereupon they conveyed Black Will into Master Arden's house, putting him into a closet at the end of his parlour. Before this they had sent

The practice to kill Arden is now set abroach.

out of the house all the servants, those excepted which were privy to the devised murder. Then went Mosby to the doors, and there stood in a night-gown of silk girded about him, and this was betwixt six and seven of the clock at night. Master Arden, having been at a neighbour's house of his named Dumpkin, and having cleared certain reckonings betwixt them, came home, and finding Mosby standing at the door asked him if it were supper-time. 'I think not,' quoth Mosby, 'it is not yet ready.' 'Then let us go and play a game at the tables in the mean season,' said Master Arden. And so they went straight into the parlour, and as they came by through the hall his wife was walking there, and Master Arden said, 'How now, Mistress Alice?' But she made small answer to him. In the meantime, one chained the wicket door of the entry. When they came into the parlour, Mosby sat down on the bench, having his face toward the place where Black Will stood. Then Michael, Master Arden's man, stood at his master's back, holding a candle in his hand to shadow Black Will, that Arden might by no means perceive him coming forth. In their play, Mosby said thus (which seemed to be the watch-word for Black Will's coming forth): 'Now may I take you, sir, if I will.' 'Take me?' quoth Master Arden. 'Which way?' With that, Black Will stepped forth and cast a towel about his neck, so to stop his breath and strangle him. Then Mosby, having at his girdle a pressing-iron of fourteen pounds weight, struck him on the head with the same, so that he fell down and gave a great groan, insomuch that they thought he had been killed.

Here the confederates join their practices.

The watch-word to the prinicipal murderer.

Then they bare him away to lay him in the countinghouse, and as they were about to lay him down, the pangs of death coming on him, he gave a great groan and stretched himself. And then Black Will gave him a great gash in the face and so killed him out of hand, laid him along, took the money out of his purse and the rings from his fingers, and then coming out of the countinghouse said, 'Now the feat is done, give me my money.' So Mistress Arden gave him ten pounds, and he coming to Greene had a horse of him, and so rode his ways. After that Black Will was gone, Mistress Arden came into the countinghouse and with a knife gave him seven or eight pricks into the breast. Then they made clean the parlour, took a clout and wiped where it was bloody, and strewed again the rushes that were shuffled with struggling, and cast the clout with which they wiped the blood and the knife that was bloody, wherewith she had wounded her husband, into a tub by the well's side, where afterwards both the same clout and knife were found. Thus this wicked woman, with her 'complices, most shamefully murdered her own husband, who most entirely loved her all his lifetime. Then she sent for two Londoners to supper, the one named Prune and the other Cole, that were grocers, which before the murder was committed were bidden to supper. When they came she said, 'I marvel where Master Arden is. We will not tarry for him, come ye and sit down, for he will not be long.' Then Mosby's sister was sent for. She came and sat down, and so they were merry.

Arden slain outright.

Black Will receiveth ten pounds for his reward of Arden's wife for murdering her husband.

After supper, Mistress Arden caused her daughter to play on the virginals, and they danced, and she with them, and so seemed to protract time, as it were, till Master Arden should

Mark what a countenance of innocence and

ignorance she
bore after the
murdering of her
husband.

come. And she said, 'I marvel where he is so long. Well, he will come anon, I am sure. I pray you, in the meanwhile let us play a game at the tables.' But the Londoners said they must go to their host's house or else they should be shut out at doors, and so, taking their leave, departed. When they were gone, the servants that were not privy to the murder were sent abroad into the town, some to seek their master and some of other errands, all saving Michael and a maid, Mosby's

The workers of
this mischief
carry out Arden
slain into the
field.

sister, and one of Mistress Arden's own daughters. Then they took the dead body and carried it out to lay it in a field next to the churchyard and joining to his garden wall, through the which he went to the church. In the meantime it began to snow, and when they came to the garden gate they remembered that they had forgotten the key, and one went in for it, and finding it, at length brought it, opened the gate, and carried the corpse into the same field, as it were ten paces from the garden gate, and laid him down on his back straight in his night-gown, with his slippers on, and between one of his slippers and his foot a long rush or two remained. When they had thus laid him down, they returned the same way they came through the garden gate into the house.

They being returned thus back again into the house the doors were opened and the servants returned home that had been

This she did to
colour her
wickedness which
by no means was
excuseable.

sent abroad, and being now very late, she sent forth her folks again to make enquiry for him in divers places, namely among the best in the town where he was wont to be, who made answer that they could tell nothing of him. Then she began to make an outcry, and said, 'Never woman had such neighbours as I have,' and herewith wept, insomuch that her neighbours came in and found her making great lamentation, pretending to marvel what was become of her husband. Where upon the mayor and others came to make search for

Arden a covetous
man and a
preferer of his
private profit
before common
gain.

him. The fair was wont to be kept partly in the town and part-ly in the Abbey, but Arden, for his own private lucre and covetous gain, had this present year procured it to be wholly kept within the Abbey ground which he had purchased, and so reaping all the gains to himself and bereaving the town of that portion which was wont to come to the inhabitants, got many a bitter curse. The mayor, going about the fair in this search, at length came to the ground where Arden lay, and as it happened, Prune the grocer getting sight of him first said, 'Stay, for methink I see one lie here.' And so they, looking and beholding the body, found that it was Master Arden lying

Arden's dead body
is described by

there thoroughly dead, and viewing diligently the manner of his body and hurts, found the rushes sticking in his slippers,

one of his
acquaintance.

and, marking further, espied certain footsteps, by reason of the snow, betwixt the place where he lay and the garden door. Then the mayor commanded every man to stay, and herewith appointed some to go about and come in at the inner side of the house through the garden as the way lay, to the place where Master Arden's dead body did lie, who all the way as they came perceived footings still before them in the snow;

Footsteps all
alongst from the
dead body of
Arden to his
dwelling house.

and so it appeared plainly that he was brought along that way from the house through the garden and so into the field where he lay. Then the mayor and his company that were with him went into the house, and knowing her evil demeanour in times past examined her of the matter. But she defied them and said, 'I would you should know I am no such woman.' Then they examined her servants, and in the examina-

A piece of
Arden's hair and
his blood spilt in
the house espied,
as also a bloody
knife and a clout
found.

tion—by reason of a piece of his hair and blood found near to the house in the way by the which they carried him forth, and likewise by the knife with which she had thrust him into the breast, and the clout wherewith they wiped the blood away which they found in the tub into the which the same were thrown—they all confessed the matter, and herself beholding her husband's blood said, 'Oh, the blood of God help, for this blood have I shed.'

Then were they all attached and committed to prison, and the mayor with others went presently to the Flower-de-Luce where they found Mosby in bed. And as they came towards him they espied his hose and purse stained with some of

Some of Arden's
blood upon
Mosby's purse.

Master Arden's blood, and when he asked what they meant by their coming in such sort they said, 'See, here ye may understand wherefore by these tokens,' showing him the blood on his hose and purse. Then he confessed the deed, and

The principals of
his murder fled
away.

so he and all the other that had conspired the murder were apprehended and laid in prison, except Greene, Black Will, and the painter, which painter and George Shakebag, that was also fled before, were never heard of. Shortly were the sessions kept at Faversham, where all the prisoners were arraigned and condemned. And thereupon being examined whether they had any other 'complices, Mistress Arden accused Brad-

Bradshaw as
unjustly accused as
his simplicity was
shamefully abused.

shaw upon occasion of the letter sent by Greene from Gravesend (as before ye have heard), which words had none other meaning but only by Bradshaw's describing of Black Will's qualities, Greene judged him a meet instrument for the execution of their pretended murder. Whereunto, notwithstanding (as Greene confessed at his death certain years after), this Bradshaw was never made privy, howbeit, he was upon this occasion of Mistress Arden immediately sent for to the sessions and indicted, and declaration made against him as a procurer of Black Will to kill Master Arden, which proceeded wholly by misunderstanding of the words contained in the letter which he brought from Greene.

Then he desired to talk with the persons condemned, and his request was granted. He therefore demanded of them if they knew him or ever had any conversation with him, and they all *Innocence no bar* said no. Then the letter being showed and read, he declared *against* the very truth of the matter and upon what occasion he told *execution.* Greene of Black Will. Nevertheless, he was condemned and suffered. These condemned persons were diversely executed in sundry places; for Michael, Master Arden's man, was hanged in chains at Faversham, and one of the maids was *Note how these* burnt there, pitifully bewailing her case, and cried out on her *malefactors* mistress that had brought her to this end, for the which she *suffered* would never forgive her. Mosby and his sister were hanged in *punishment.* Smithfield at London. Mistress Arden was burned at Canterbury the four and twentieth of March. Greene came again certain years after, was apprehended, condemned, and hanged in chains in the highway between Ospring and Boughton-*Black Will burnt* against-Faversham. Black Will was burnt on a scaffold at *at Flushing.* Flushing in Zealand. Adam Fowle, that dwelt at the Flower-de-Luce in Faversham was brought into trouble about this matter, and carried up to London with his legs bound under the horse's belly, and committed to prison in the Marshalsea, for that Mosby was heard to say, 'Had it not been for Adam Fowle, I had not come to this trouble,' meaning that the bringing of the silver dice for a token to him from Mistress Arden, as ye have heard, occasioned him to renew familiarity with her again. But when the matter was thoroughly ripped up, and that Mosby had cleared him, protesting that he was never of knowledge in any behalf to the murder, the man's innocence preserved him.

A Wonder This one thing seemed very strange and notable touching *touching the* Master Arden, that in the place where he was laid, being *print of Arden's* dead, all the proportion of his body might be seen two years *dead body two* after and more so plain as could be, for the grass did not grow *years after he* where his body had touched, but between his legs, between *was slain.* his arms, and about the hollowness of his neck, and round about his body; and where his legs, arms, head, or any other part of his body had touched, no grass growed at all of all that time, so that many strangers came in that meantime, beside the townsmen, to see the print of his body there on the ground in that field, which field he had (as some have reported), most cruelly taken from a woman that had been a widow to one Cooke, and after married to one Richard Read, a mariner, to the great hindrance of her and her husband, the said Read; for they had long enjoyed it by a lease which they had of it for many years, not then expired. Nevertheless, he got it from them, for the which the said Read's wife not only exclaimed against him in shedding many a salt tear, but also cursed him most bitterly even to his face, wishing many a vengeance to light upon him, and that all the world might *God heareth the* wonder on him. Which was thought then to come to pass *tears of the* when he was thus murdered and lay in that field from mid- *oppressed and* night till the morning, and so all that day, being the fair day *taketh vengeance:* till night; all the which day there were many hundreds of peo- *note an example* ple came wondering about him. And thus far touching this *in Arden.* horrible and heinous murder of Master Arden.